ACKNOWLEDGEMENT

I wish to thank Goli Bakhtiar for her invaluable help and encouragement in writing this story about her cousin, Soraya. The unpublished information that Goli was able to give has made a big difference to the previous, undisclosed details around Soraya's divorce from the Shah of Persia.

"A good title that is 100% true. After the divorce,
the Shah was no longer loved by the public."
Goli Bakhtiar

CONTENTS

ACKNOWLEDGEMENT   vii
PROLOGUE   xvii

1   THREE FAMILIES   1
     The Pahlavi Family   1
     The Bakhtiari Family   4
     The Karl Family   5

2   A MIXED MARRIAGE   7
     Isfahan, Persia, 1923   7
     A Chance Encounter   9
     The New Shah   10
     Pahlavi–Bakhtiari Friction   12

3   TO BERLIN AND RETURN   13
     Berlin, 1933–37   13
     Return to Isfahan   16
     An Arranged Marriage   19

4	WWII IN IRAN	21
	A Three-Week Defeat	21
	Reza Shah Deposed	23
	School in Isfahan	24
5	RETURN TO EUROPE	27
	Schooling in Switzerland	27
	London, 1950	29
	Trouble for the Shah	30
	The Snapshot	31
	Paris Interlude	32
	Palace Intrigue	33
6	SORAYA MEETS THE SHAH	35
	Preparation	35
	Reception	36
	Courtship and Doubt	39
	Postponement of Wedding	41
7	THE WEDDING OF THE DECADE	44
	The Dress	45
	Panic	45
	Marriage Ceremony	47
	Reception	49
	Mounting Crisis	51
8	POLITICAL PROBLEMS	52
	Mosaddeq and the Nationalists	52
	Mosaddeq Post-WWII	53
	The Tudeh and the Fedayeen	55
	Assassination	56

9	THE INDECISIVE SHAH	58
	Court Intrigue	58
	Morteza Yazdan-Panah	58
	The Shah's Psychological Pillars	59
	Ernest Peron	60
	Asadollah Alam	61
	Princess Ashraf	63
10	LIVING WITH THE PAHLAVIS	66
	The Echtessassi Palace	66
	Loneliness	68
	Holiday with the Shah	70
	Nimtaj Molouk	70
	Princess Shams	72
	Ali Reza Pahlavi	72
	Other Minor Relatives	73
	Princess Shahnaz	74
11	THE INNOCENT EMPRESS	75
	The Rude Awakening	75
	Tainted Holiday	76
	Early Troubles with Mosaddeq	78
12	THE MOSADDEQ AFFAIR	80
	Time Magazine's Man of the Year	80
	Timeline of Events	81
	Soraya Leaves Iran	86
13	FLEEING IRAN	88
	Soraya's Decisiveness	88
	CIA Involvement	90

14	ESCAPE TO ROME	93
	Baghdad, Sunday, 16th August 1953	93
	Rome, Monday, 17th August 1953	95
	Parsimonious Future	96
	Rome, Thursday, 20th August 1953	100
	Rome, Friday, 21st August 1953	101
	Return to Tehran	101
	Mosaddeq's Reprieve	102
	Settlement	103
15	SORAYA'S POPULARITY PEAKS	105
	Doubts – Revenge or Justice	105
	Wants for Nothing	106
	The Soraya Foundation	108
	A New-Found Sport	110
	A Fear of Flying	110
	Iran's Regeneration	111
	Assassination Attempt	111
	Court Formality Relaxed	112
	Order of Chivalry	113
16	THE DARK CLOUD	114
	The Beginning of the End	114
	The Trip Abroad	116
	New York	117
	Washington	118
	California	118
	Los Angeles	119
	Florida	120
17	EUROPE	121
	England	121

	West Germany	124
	The Shah's Paranoia	125
	Royal Matchmaker	127
18	THE JEWEL IN THE CROWN	129
	India	129
	Turkey	132
	King Saud	132
	Soviet Union	133
19	THE DIVORCE	135
	The Slow Build-up Accelerates	135
	Whispers	136
	Madame Claude	137
	Ultimatum	138
	Soraya Resolute	139
	The End of the Fairy Tale	141
	The Forlorn Hope Delegation	142
	Princess Gabriella of Savoy	144
20	RUMOURS AND FALSEHOODS	145
	So-called Impeccable Sources	145
21	AFTERMATH OF DIVORCE	151
	A New Beginning	151
	The Divorce Settlement	152
	Queen Farah Diba	154
	The Nobel 200	155
	Shah's Popularity Plummets Further	156
22	MALE FRIENDSHIPS	158
	Prince Johannes von Thurn	158

Maximilian Schell   159
Gunter Sachs   160
Prince Raimondo Orsini   161
Hugh O'Brian   162
Other Affairs   163
Countless Interviews   163

23   THE THREE FACES OF A WOMAN   165
Dino de Laurentis   165
Franco Indovina   166
The Three Faces   167
A Teenager at Last   170

24   SIX HAPPY YEARS   172
Life with Franco   172
May 1972 – Disaster   173
Who Were "They"?   174
Aftershock   176
Paris   178
Audouin de Barbot   178

25   THE SHAH'S DOWNFALL   181

26   THE CLOSING YEARS   187
The Shah Dies   187
Khalil Dies   189
Shah's Tomb   189
Loved Twice?   190

27   THE FINAL YEARS   192
The Rapid Decline   192
Sudden Death   193

CONTENTS

The Auction   195

Controversial Will   196

28   POSSIBLE OR PROBABLE   198

BIBLIOGRAPHY   200

APPENDIX
Realisation (Of the Will)   206

PROLOGUE

'I think you were in love with her.'

I looked at the small, gentle-looking, elderly lady who had come to me at the end of my talk on Queen Soraya. She held a copy of my novel, *The World is Empty*, which she wanted me to sign.

I smiled at her as I wrote *Best Wishes* and asked for her name.

'Harriet,' she replied.

'I never met her, you know. Can you fall in love with someone by simply seeing their photograph?'

'Oh yes,' she asserted. 'I saw the man who was to become my husband in a press photo, and it changed the course of my life for ever. He was a policeman who had saved a youngster from drowning in the River Severn and the article described he was a local bobby at Iron-Bridge. At the time, I lived with my parents in the adjacent village of Coalport, a few miles away. He became my first and only boyfriend, and we were happily married for almost sixty years.'

'That's wonderful,' I replied as I handed the signed book back to her. 'I hope you enjoy this story, but I'm afraid it doesn't have a happy-ever-after ending.' She gave me a sweet smile and left to allow the next lady to approach me with another book to sign.

The Much Wenlock Ladies Luncheon Club had been a delightful

audience at their monthly meeting in The Raven Hotel, asking many questions about what happened after Queen Soraya's divorce from the Shah of Persia. It had been a considerable contrast to my usual morning talks, typically weekly, to men's Probus Clubs where I was sometimes lucky to get a cup of coffee.

Occasionally, events in our lives leave unforgettable memories. Some are sufficiently strong that we can remember exactly where we experienced them and their date. The most sensational events are totally unexpected and instantly hit the international headlines. While alighting from a bus in St Anne's Square, near Blackpool, a stranger boarding the bus said, 'The Russians have shot Kennedy.' I have never forgotten learning about the American President's assassination on 22nd November 1963; it was 7.30pm, just one hour after the event in Dallas, Texas.

Other events tend to be more of national importance, rather than international. I met the local primary school's headmaster on my way home, after playing in a badminton match at Castletown, Isle of Man. It was 6th February 1958. He told me Manchester United's plane had crashed at Munich, an hour and a half earlier.

Some incidents are purely personal. On 21st March 1958, I was seventeen and never forgot my girlfriend, Anne, telling me in the school playground that the Shah of Persia had divorced Queen Soraya because she couldn't have a baby. She asked, would I have divorced her for the same reason, if we were married? Our teenage romance was to peter out some years later when we attended different universities. For weeks after the announcement of the divorce, the newspapers were full of photographs of Soraya, expressing sympathy for her dilemma. The years went by, but I never forgot her elegance and beauty – comparable with Grace Kelly or Ingrid Bergman.

In 2009, my first novel, *A Nastia Game*, was published. Set in Iraq, the story was based on my experience of designing a computer wargame for training RAF and overseas air force officers in the art of air warfare at the RAF Staff College, Bracknell. At the time, in the mid-1970s, I was the college's computer systems analyst, specialising in weapons simulation. The wargame software was subsequently sold by the Ministry of Defence to Iraq in 1978; it was probably misused to plan Iraq's invasion of Iran in 1980.

While researching material for *A Nastia Game*, I had come across an article in *The Times* online, dated 14th March 2006. Its headline: *MP's cloak and dagger mission: ask Dr Germ about Iraq's weapons.* The report claimed Ian Gibson, a Member of Parliament for Norwich North, had flown to the Middle East to identify one of his former students, Rihab Taha. Gibson had supervised Taha's PhD on plant toxins at the University of East Anglia. Known as Dr Germ by the British press, she had been Saddam Hussein's senior biological weapons expert and a member of Saddam's Command Revolutionary Council. Recently released, after thirty months in Abu Graib jail, where she had been held prisoner by the Americans, she had continually protested she was an agent for the British Secret Service during the Iran–Iraq war from 1980 to 1988.

The article gave me the idea to have an attractive, female MI6 spy as the central character in *A Nastia Game*. Remembering Soraya's mysterious beauty, she became my double agent based on a real "*Mata Hari*" – Rihab Taha.

After the novel's publication, I began giving talks about my novel to societies such as the University of the 3rd Age, the National Trust, and local historical societies. When I described the story's heroine as looking like Queen Soraya, a murmur frequently went around the room.

The audience was remembering her exquisite presence, her fairy-tale, teenage marriage to the Shah of Iran, and their subsequent divorce. However, few knew of Soraya's heartbreaking, sad life that was to trigger the undoing of the Shah, and end with her mysterious death in a Paris penthouse. After the talk, the first question asked by the audience was invariably, 'Whatever happened to Soraya?' As the years passed, I researched further Soraya's history. I developed a talk on her life, now given to over fifty societies. However, there is a world of difference between the material for a fifty-minute, illustrated presentation and a comprehensive biography. *Queen Soraya, The Divorce that Destroyed a Dynasty* is the result of many years research. It includes previously unpublished material gathered from corresponding with two of Soraya's cousins, one living in Spain and the other in Iran.

Courtesy Getty
Elegance, beauty, beguiling, simplicity

1

THREE FAMILIES

The Pahlavi Family

Reza Khan was born in September 1878 to a Persian Major, Abbas Ali Khan, and a Georgian Muslim mother, Noush-Afarin. Her family had fled to Persia after Persia's Caucasian territories of Georgia and Armenia were ceded to Russia following the Russo-Persian War of 1826–28. They lived in Abbas Ali Khan's home village of Alasht, a small hamlet located in the northern foothills of the Alborz Mountains, south of the Caspian Sea. Abbas Ali Khan was an officer in the 7th Iranian Regiment, but he died suddenly when Reza was only two months old.

The winter of 1878 was exceptionally cold. Consequently, Noush decided to leave Alasht with her baby boy and travel 150 miles over the mountains to Tehran where it would be warmer. She planned to stay with her brother and look for a job. In a snowstorm, travelling with a caravan of fellow pilgrims, they stopped at an inn to eat and change horses. In the bitter freezing temperatures, the baby had stopped breathing and was declared dead by the caravan's guide. With Noush crying bitterly, the guide explained they had to restart the journey immediately for fear of being trapped in the heavy snow; they could not wait to bury the child. Weeping hysterically, Noush gave her son to the innkeeper and asked him to bury Reza. The owner agreed he would, after the snow had stopped.

The innkeeper put the child, wrapped in a blanket, near the inn's fireplace. An hour or so later, the innkeeper, on a galloping horse, caught up with the caravan. He told Noush that as soon as the baby had warmed up, it had started to cry. The baby was to become the Shah of Persia – Reza Shah Pahlavi. The story passed into Persian folklore as being true. It undoubtedly helps to explain Reza's mystifyingly rapid advancement from commoner to shah.

Noush returned to the inn on the back of the innkeeper's horse. A week later, after Reza had fully recovered, she eventually reached her brother's house with her baby boy. She remarried a year later and left Reza to be brought up by his uncle. In 1882, his uncle sent Reza to a family friend, Amir Kazim Khan, an officer in the Persian Cossack Brigade. There, Reza was educated by Amir Kazim's children's private tutor.

When Reza Khan was sixteen, he joined the ranks of the Cossack Brigade, which was mostly commanded by Russian officers. In 1896, when only eighteen, he married his cousin, Maryam Savadkoohi. Maryam died in February 1903, soon after giving birth to a daughter, Hamdam Saltaneh Khan. By the age of thirty-two, in 1910, Reza had been commissioned in the brigade. Rapid promotion followed. Although most of the brigade's senior officers were still Russian, by 1916 Reza was a major, having married his second wife, Nimtaj, the daughter of General Teymour Khan Ayromlou. The marriage was reputedly arranged and proved an advantage in Reza Khan's military career. Marrying the boss's daughter accelerated his advance in the Cossack hierarchy.

The Persian Qajar dynasty had wished to remain neutral in World War One (WWI). However, in 1914 the country was quickly occupied by the Allies – the Russians in the north and the British in the south.

The Persian resistance to the Allies' invasion had lasted less than a month. The Cossack Brigade was co-opted into the allied forces and fought against the Ottoman Empire, helping to secure Russian interests in eastern Turkey. The British exploited the southern oil fields around the Persian Gulf, while the Russians occupied the northern oil fields in Azerbaijan, then a province of Persia.

Following the Russian Revolution of 1917, the new Soviet Union became neutral. As a result, the British took control of the Cossack Brigade. The Soviet officers were removed and replaced for the duration of the war with either British or trusted Persian officers – one of whom was Lieutenant Colonel Reza Khan, whose wife, Nimtaj, had given him a daughter, Shams.

When WWI finished, the British withdrew from Persia. However, the Soviets remained in oil-rich Azerbaijan. The Persian Shah, Ahmad Qajar, ordered the Cossack Brigade, now under Brigadier Reza Khan's command, to regain control of his fractured country. Despite crushing various separatist and dissident movements, Azerbaijan was a step too far. It became a Soviet Socialist Republic.

In October 1919, Nimtaj gave birth to twins, a girl, Ashraf, and a boy, Mohammed. Reza Khan was seen by the masses as the man who could save the country from future chaos. Encouraged by the Majlis, the elected Persian Government, he led a bloodless coup, seized the capital, and began enlarging the Persian army to over 40,000 men.

By 1923, Reza Khan's enigmatic, powerful personality persuaded the Majlis that he should become Prime Minister. In 1925, he removed Shah Ahmad Qajar, sending him into exile in France; the Qajar dynasty had ruled for almost 200 years. The Majlis declared Reza Khan the new Shah on 12ᵗʰ December 1925. He was crowned Shah Reza Pahlavi in April 1926. He adopted the dynastic name Pahlavi as it was the title given to an unbeatable, champion wrestler – a pahlavan. Furthermore, he also declared his son was the Crown Prince; Mohammed Reza Pahlavi was aged six.

With control of the Persian government, Reza Shah began a programme of modernisation. Centralisation became the name of the game. Large road-building projects were undertaken. The trans-Iranian railway to connect the Persian Gulf with the Caspian Sea began, comprehensive education for all was introduced, and increased women's rights removed the need to wear the veil. Industrialisation multiplied ten-fold.

The Bakhtiari Family

The Bakhtiaris were the descendants of an ancient nomadic tribe that ruled an area of the Zagros Mountains to the southwest of Isfahan, roughly the size of Wales. Greek historians who accompanied Alexander the Great with his army into Persia between 330BC and 323BC referred to a tribe in the southwest as the "Bakteris". The name Bakhtiari means "the people of the West". They had their own language, Lori, based on ancient Persian, and they would, from time to time, form alliances with other neighbouring tribes. Such loose confederations had frequently been seen as a threat to the central authorities in Tehran. Although there is no evidence that the Bakhtiaris ever had designs on the Persian throne, their relationship with Tehran's authorities had remained amenable until the reign of Neder Shah, 1736 to 1747. Thousands of Bakhtiaris were then exiled to the far eastern border of Persia with Afghanistan. There, they were conscripted into the army to fight rebellions on the Indian border. In 1746, Ali Saleh-Bakhtiar successfully commanded Neder Shah's campaign in Kandahar. Today, there are still Bakhtiari families, descendants from those soldiers, living in Afghanistan and Pakistan.

By 1870, Esfandiar-Bakhtiar Khan, the Bakhtiari clan leader, as a result of backing from friendly tribes, had become powerful and rich, owning vast estates in Khuzestan, the most southwestern province of

Persia. The Qajar government in Tehran, possibly apprehensive that he could make a bid for the throne, planned his assassination. In 1882, he was shot at Isfahan. His two sons, one of whom was also Esfandiar-Khan, were imprisoned for seven years. However, the setback did not prevent the Bakhtiaris' wealth and influence growing.

The source of their wealth lay with abandoning their nomadic lifestyle by fortifying villages. The numerous Bakhtiari clans dug wells and cultivated the land. The products from their farms flooded the markets of Isfahan, Shiraz, Qom and Tehran. The family soon became successful importers of goods from Europe and Russia.

The navigable River Karun flowed through Bakhtiari land before reaching the Persian Gulf. Travellers had to pay a toll to cross their bridges in exchange for protection. When, in 1904, Esfandiar-Bakhtiar Khan junior was approached by a delegation of Englishmen seeking to drill for oil on his land, he demanded a 10% share of the profits. Bitter negotiations dragged on for several years, whilst unproductive drilling proceeded. He died in 1907 – the year oil was discovered in Khuzestan, near Abadan.

The Bakhtiari clan eventually agreed a 10% share of the profits in 1909 when the Anglo-Bakhtiari Oil Company was set up. It made them the wealthiest family in Persia.

The Karl Family

Gottlieb Karl was a gunsmith in Thuringia, a small state in eastern central Germany. In 1860, the Russian Czar, Alexander II, contracted him to build and manage a rifle factory in St Petersburg. There, he fathered a son, Franz, who was educated to be bilingual with dual nationality. After engineering training, Franz worked in his father's munitions factory and married a Baltic German, Alma Selmer, who had been brought up in Latvia – a Russian dependency. Franz proved to be a gifted engineer and in his early twenties was appointed the head representative for two giant German engineering companies to the Russian Imperial Court – AEG, an electrical goods producer, and BASF, a chemical manufacturer. Franz and Alma had three children – a son, also Franz, and two daughters, Eva and Barbara. Eva was born in Moscow in 1906, where she spent the first eight years of her life. She became fluent in Russian as well as German.

When WWI began, Russia and Germany were enemies and in October 1914, the Karls were banished, along with hundreds of other German internees, to Moldovia. Lodged in log cabins, they were subjected to curfews but kept warm and had sufficient food. When the November 1917 revolution began, and the newly formed Soviet Union declared itself neutral, it was an opportunity for the Karls and several other German families to flee west. With a horse-drawn cart, they travelled north-west towards the Baltic, a thousand miles away. Occasionally, they had to hide for several weeks from sporadic outbreaks of violence between rival factions that eventually led to the civil war between the Bolsheviks and the White Russians. Franz and his family arrived in Riga soon after the signing of the Brest-Litovsk Treaty in March 1918 – the armistice that officially ended hostilities between the Bolsheviks and Germany. The Karls travelled to Berlin by train where the managing director of AEG rented an apartment for Franz's family. The three children started school, and they quickly adjusted to their new environment. Alma and Franz could not have imagined that one day they would become grandparents to the Queen of Persia.

2

A MIXED MARRIAGE

Isfahan, Persia, 1923

The First World War in Europe and Mesopotamia had finished and the subsequent Versailles Peace Conference of 1919 had changed the geographical boundaries of the Middle East beyond recognition. The Ottoman Empire had been annihilated. From the Ottoman's former lands in Arabia, the British had created three new countries – Palestine, Transjordan and Iraq, while the French – Syria and Lebanon. The Soviet Union had annexed Armenia and Georgia from the Ottomans, while Azerbaijan was now one of their socialist republics. The August 1920 Treaty of Sevres had originally allocated parts of Turkey to Italy and Greece. However, led by Kemal Atatürk, the Turkish army, the rump composed of former Ottoman troops, reconquered much of their land after a three-year war. At the April 1923 Conference of Lausanne, the League of Nations recognised Atatürk's' sectarian state of Turkey.

The stringent conditions imposed on Germany at Versailles – losing the Alsace and Lorraine to France, and control of their African colonies – was deeply resented by the Germans who, by 1923, were already secretly rearming. The Germans' secret ambitions to regain their lost territories would become public when the Hitler-Ludendorff Putsch occurred in November. If a second war was to occur, oil would be a major factor in victory as mechanisation would be much greater than in WWI.

The largest oilfields in Asia were at Abadan, southwest Persia, in a province largely controlled by the Bakhtiari clan. The British had begun negotiating with the Bakhtiaris as early as 1904 to explore for oil on their lands. When commercial quantities were discovered in 1907, the British negotiated a working relationship with the Bakhtiaris to extract the oil. The British needed to purchase the land and acquire a trusted workforce to protect their refineries. An acceptable, financial, long-term settlement with the Bakhtiaris was necessary. In April 1909, the Anglo-Bakhtiari Oil Company (ABOC) was formed with a share capital of £400,000. The Bakhtiaris owned 10% of the shares. Some months later, it was merged into the much larger Anglo-Persian Oil Company (APOC). By 1912, the APOC had become largely owned by the British Government – today's forerunner of British Petroleum (BP). The Bakhtiaris received 3% of the APOC's profits but obtained extra sums in dividends. The Bakhtiaris were, therefore, motivated to safeguard the interests of the Company.

The British, with Indian troops, had invaded southern Persia in 1914, at the beginning of WWI, to protect the APOC's fields. Meanwhile, the northern oilfields in the Persian province of Azerbaijan were seized by the Russian allies. The British troops withdrew from Persia in 1919, but the supposedly neutral Soviet Union, formed after their 1917 revolution, remained in Azerbaijan. An attempt by the Persian army to regain their territory was unsuccessful.

The daughter of one of the Bakhtiari Clan's leaders, who had negotiated the formation of the ABOC with the British in 1907, was Bibi Maryam Bakhtiar, the second wife of Esfandiar-Bakhtiar Khan junior. They had two boys: Montazem, the eldest, and Khalil, born in 1901. Maryam was sufficiently shrewd to realise that, if a second war occurred, the clan's profitable arrangement could be in danger. She, therefore, decided to send her two sons to the two different sides of the probable conflict.

She explained her worries to her two sons that it was essential to be ahead in the game so they would be ready to negotiate with either the British or the Germans if they invaded Persia for their oil.

Montazem was sent to London University while Khalil went to Berlin University, both to study politics.

Khalil, aged twenty-two, was accompanied to Berlin by his half-brother, Hormoz – the son of Esfandiar-Bakhtiar Khan junior's fourth wife. The cosmopolitan atmosphere of Berlin was altogether different from Qajar Shah's Persia, where women still wore the veil. Both young men took to the lifestyle and enjoyed socialising. The young German women were usually blonde, unlike those from Persia. Khalil reputedly had much success attracting the girls, as his dark, swarthy skin and deep, hypnotic brown eyes tended to be the antithesis of fair-haired German boys.

A Chance Encounter

At a student party, Khalil met a blue-eyed, blonde girl, aged eighteen, called Eva Karl. Their meeting was to become a perfect example of love at first sight. Their relationship would become permanent – it would last all their lives. They courted throughout their first academic year, sufficient time for them to realise they wanted to marry. Knowing that a marriage to a German Christian would not be accepted by his family, Khalil returned to Isfahan to seek his mother's permission, and that of his guardian – an uncle. In June 1925, without their consent, Khalil returned to marry Eva. It was conducted by a local Imam according to Muslim rites in her parent's house in Westfailische Strasse. It was a remarkable event – a Protestant Christian, not yet having reached the age of majority, marrying a Muslim Shia, albeit a secular one. No one from Khalil's family attended except his half-brother, Hormoz, who acted as best man. After Eva and Khalil had graduated from university, they moved to Isfahan in 1928, during which time the Qajar dynasty had fallen and been replaced by the first Pahlavi Shah.

Isfahan, the birthplace of Khalil, was the epicentre of the Bakhtiari clan. It also contained a sizeable German community. Consequently, Khalil and Eva soon settled and began to plan a family. They began renovating a house. Common German architectural features were incorporated that puzzled the locals, such as central heating and double glazing.

Isfahan's German community was known to contain agents who, with the help of a small clique of rebel Bakhtiaris, were occasionally wrecking the APOC's pipelines. Ironically, the British were paying a different group of Bakhtiaris to police and protect the oil installations. The insurgents were, therefore, heightening the tension between Reza Shah Pahlavi's government, the moderate members of the Bakhtiari clan, and the British.

On the 22nd June 1932, Soraya was born in the English Missionary Hospital in Isfahan – a beautiful girl with green eyes. The Persian tradition believed that the first-born should be a boy, thereby conferring honour on the father in the male-dominated society. However, for the enlightened couple, the custom was unimportant as Soraya was a healthy child, born on their sixth wedding anniversary. The previous evening, the sky had been dominated by the constellation Pleiades, commonly called "seven rays" – in Farsi, "soraya". The girl, weighing eight pounds and ten ounces, was bonny and healthy. Her parents were ecstatic, but a storm was approaching over the horizon.

The New Shah

During Khalil's absence from Persia, the 200-year-old Qajar dynasty had been removed and replaced by Shah Reza Pahlavi. The Government, the Majlis, had declared Reza Pahlavi the Shah in December 1925. The following April, Reza declared his first son the Crown Prince and heir. Prince Mohammed Pahlavi was just six years of age.

Reza Shah's policies attempted to bring Persia into the twentieth century. He removed the Imam's influence on society by introducing a western educational system with co-educational schools. He established the University of Tehran – Persia's first. He created a modern economic structure with banks, telecommunications, and high street stores employing women. By encouraging women to remove the veil, he believed Persian society would advance towards modernisation. The north-south railway was given high priority. A modern judiciary system was fashioned along European lines.

The shift from a rural, agricultural economy of local bazaars run by the tribal system, where the masses were uneducated, to an urban industrial system was not universally popular. Opposition to the Shah was not so much from the landed, wealthy upper classes as from the Imams whose strength lay with the rural hoi polloi who were loyal to their religious teachings. A conflict was inevitable.

When Khalil and Eva had arrived in Isfahan in 1928, Reza Shah's centralisation policy was accelerating. The wearing of western clothes was becoming common. Public places, such as cinemas and restaurants, allowed women. Mosques used chairs instead of kneeling on the floor. In many provinces, uprisings by the tribes, encouraged by the Muslim clerics, took place. In the southwest, many of the Bakhtiaris, believing Pahlavi to be an upstart, joined the revolt.

The post-WWI German government had courted Persia by offering technical aid and training while suggesting the Persian people were Aryan. This suggestion boosted Pahlavi's delusions of grandeur, and, believing the idea much superior than the hitherto belief that Persians were a mix of Arabs and Indians, he made the use of the word "Iran" de rigueur. Reza Shah, very much pro-German, asked the League of Nations to use the term Iran. By the 1930s, he had become an admirer of Adolf Hitler. He saw them both as having risen from the ranks to become notable leaders of their countries.

The name Persia had originally been derived from the province of Pars where the common language of Parsi, now known as Farsi, was spoken. The ancient Greeks referred to the entire country as Pars, which, at the time, was Persia's centre of political power. Today, Farsi is the official language of Iran.

Pahlavi–Bakhtiari Friction

Shah Pahlavi needed money to modernise Iranian society. Increasing taxes was insufficient. The existence of oil on Bakhtiari territory had exacerbated Reza Pahlavi's determination to undermine the tribe's influence within the APOC. The participation of some of the clan's rebel members blowing-up pipelines gave him the excuse he needed.

In 1928, the British-run APOC was ordered to negotiate with the Tehran government. It resulted in the Bakhtiaris being forced to sell their shares to the Tehran government. Some Bakhtiaris were arrested and put on trial. Twelve were executed by firing squad for supporting the Imams' revolt. Bakhtiari territory was divided up. Bakhtiari chiefs were ordered to exchange their land with properties in other provinces. A diaspora of the Bakhtiaris saw their right to use their Bakhtiari name on their passports removed. Consequently, they chose ancestors' names such as Zafar, Esfandiar, and Assad.

Khalil kept a low profile during the troubles. Being a minor in the clan's hierarchy, his inheritance was a relatively small holding – a village south of Isfahan called Gafarog. With Reza Pahlavi persecuting and imprisoning so many of his clan, he realised Eva would be safer back in Germany. In February 1933, with Soraya only eight months old, Eva and Soraya left for Germany. Khalil told Eva he could not leave Iran immediately but would follow as soon as possible.

3

TO BERLIN AND RETURN

Berlin, 1933–37

For Eva, alone with Soraya, it was a long, tiring journey in the height of the winter. The trip took them to the port of Bandar Anzali on the Caspian Sea, by boat to Baku, and two train journeys to Berlin via Moscow. They stayed with Eva's parents. Nonetheless, Eva looked forward to the move, as for five years she had struggled with the hot summer climate in Isfahan, typically averaging 36°C, so different from Moscow, where she had been born, with the summer average of 23°C.

Reza Shah's reasons for imposing restrictions on the Bakhtiaris were several. Firstly, their semi-autonomy in the Zagros Mountains and their agreement with the British to protect the oil pipelines troubled the central government. Secondly, their holding of shares in the original ABOC that were subsumed into the APOC was not in line with consolidating all Iranian oil shares into a single government purse.

Having been coerced into surrendering their shares to the Government, younger Bakhtiaris were conscripted for army duties on the eastern Afghan border. The British/Bakhtiari relationship troubled the Shah so much that it gave him an excuse for mass arrests. Being pro-German, he shut his eyes to the growing number of German agents creeping into the country as so-called technicians to work on infrastructure projects. He believed the Axis powers would be victorious in a probable Second World War – a belief that would finally lose him his throne. Seeing the problems, Khalil hastily put his business affairs in order to join his wife and daughter in Berlin, less than six months after they had left Isfahan.

Eva and Khalil rented a four-room apartment in Nestorstrausse, in the leafy suburbs on the west side of Berlin, near the university. Khalil had to register with the police. He claimed he was a farmer because his family owned land and farms in Persia. His preference to be registered as a Khan – a hereditary title for a landowner from an aristocratic family – was brushed aside. There was no such profession in Germany.

During the family's stay in Berlin, Soraya became inseparable from her grandfather. By the age of one, she was walking and soon speaking good German. Every Sunday, he would take her out to play in the parks, go sailing on the lakes at Potsdam, or visit the nearby zoo. Franz Karl recalled that she was choosy and would not play with everyone. She would scrutinise the children, especially the boys; it wasn't long before she was ordering even the bigger children about. He remembers Soraya was quite fearless, and gave an example. 'I remember a walk through the Grunewald, a forested area on the west side of the city, when a huge black dog pursued us. His wild looks and violent barking quite frightened me. However, Soraya ran towards him and put her arms around his neck. I was terrified. There wasn't any need. The dog and Soraya immediately became friends.'

From her childhood Soraya had a great love of animals. In her home she looked after a yellow canary and a mischievous black-and-white fox terrier. She particularly remembered a party at one of Berlin's lakes. There was a shooting gallery, sack racing and an egg and spoon race. There was also an open-air theatre where she played

Sleeping Beauty. Her role consisted solely of being awakened from her one-hundred-year sleep by the young prince's kiss. An experience she presumably found pleasant.

Unafraid of strangers, she would approach them in the park, stand in front of them, her green eyes asking, 'Am I not beautiful?' Everyone would smile and ask, 'What's your name?' and then pay her compliments. Satisfied she had their attention, she would move on.

Her first language was German, whether with her grandparents or at *Kindergarten*. However, Khalil, fluent in German himself, insisted teaching her Lori – the language of the Bakhtiaris.

Furthermore, Eva and Soraya's grandfather taught her Russian as an intellectual exercise. As early as four years of age, she was effectively trilingual. Years later, she was able to converse in Russian when she met Nikita Khrushchev and sat next to him at the Bolshoi Ballet.

The stay in Berlin was uneventful for Khalil, as he was unable to get work apart from giving private lessons teaching Iranian. However, he was beginning to become aware of the political situation in Europe, which he hoped would go away. In 1936, it affected him personally. Hitler announced a general conscription for all men living in Germany between the ages of 18 and 45 – irrespective of their nationality. Everywhere, the talk was of war.

Khalil faced stark choices. On the one hand, refuse and be sent to an internment camp, or return to Iran and hope the persecution of the Bakhtiaris had lessened. He had been keeping in touch with his family, but money transfers from his Iranian bank to Berlin had become unreliable. Furthermore, as the German Mark strengthened, the exchange rate had plummeted.

When Khalil received his army call-up papers, there was only one solution. In despair, Eva agreed to return to Isfahan, despite being seven months pregnant. Tearfully, Soraya said goodbye to her grandfather, whom she would not see for ten years. They travelled by train to Moscow and thence to Astrakhan on the Caspian Sea. Two ship journeys then took them back to Bandar Anzali – a total distance of approximately 3,000 miles that took ten days. It was upsetting for Eva having to leave her native Berlin for the second time. Whereas many marriages would have crumbled under the strain, her love for Khalil knew no bounds; she would have made any sacrifice for him. Soraya remembered very little of the journey, except catching occasional glimpses of the wide River Volga from the train.

Return to Isfahan

When the family reached Isfahan, however, they were not welcomed by the anti-Bakhtiari government officials. Khalil was put under curfew by the authorities and could not leave the environs of Isfahan without a police permit. All suspect clans, especially the Bakhtiaris, were being monitored. Apart from this inconvenience, Khalil was left in peace for he was considered a relatively minor member of the clan. Anticipating their arrival from Berlin, Bibi Maryam, Khalil's mother, had had their rented house prepared in readiness for Eva to give birth. A boy, Bijan, was born on 15th October 1937. Bijan was chubby, blond and full of life.

Khalil worked to improve their house. In the gardens he planted fruit trees and built a small, round pond for paddling during the hot summer. The house became a mix of Persian and European characteristics. It was a comfortable home for the young family and their two dogs – a German shepherd and a greyhound, bought to please Soraya and satisfy her love of dogs. The house was equipped with wood-burning stoves to supply central heating. It also had a bath with running hot and cold water, which was a rare luxury in Iran.

As Khalil worked, watched by Soraya, he began to tell her stories of his own father, Esfandiar Khan. She was intrigued to discover that he had had five wives. Consequently, Khalil had numerous cousins, many of whom he hadn't met and didn't know their names. Each wife had their own house. Khalil explained the wives had all been well looked after, but some had been divorced after a short time while others, including his mother's marriage, had lasted for over thirty years.

Soraya found this practice a peculiarly bizarre, unfair arrangement and began asking the family's two maids if their fathers had several wives. She was to discover that it was common for future couples never to have seen each other until after they were married. At the ceremony, the fiancée would wear a veil that hid both her face and figure. She was not allowed to look up to see her future husband's face. If the couple found they didn't love each other, then the male could divorce his wife, in which case a pre-arranged financial compensation would be paid to his ex-wife's parents.

For five years, Soraya had seen her parents and German grandparents living a happy, monogamous relationship. It was an ethic that Soraya would believe was correct for the rest of her life. Unknowingly, not only would this belief affect the major, future event of her life, but kick-off a lingering doubt in her mind – was she German or Iranian?

Soraya attended a small, private school at the bottom of the garden run by a German, Mrs Mantel. She made friends with the other half-dozen or so children, mostly her age; the children's' parents were mostly German engineers modernising Iran's factories. Soraya learnt to count, write and enjoy reading both French and German texts. She learnt to play the piano. On each of the children's birthdays, Mrs Mantel would bake them cakes. Christmas was celebrated with a decorated tree. They would sing Christmas carols such as "Silent Night". Soraya admitted in her biography she felt a Christian. Her mother on such occasions would get homesick and, with sadness in her eyes, talk about "back there". As the only child at school with an Iranian father, Soraya was confused about her nationality and admitted that at times she felt lonely.

Soraya's relationship with her father was something of an enigma. She acknowledged in her first biography she was afraid of her father. However, she added that he was a good man who did not bother her much. He left both his children's education entirely to Eva, an arrangement common in Iran.

Whenever they could, the young family would spend time in Gafarog, a village in the foothills of the Zagros Mountains. There, the cooler climate suited Eva. Soraya and her brother would play in the surrounding forest. Soraya learnt to fish – a pursuit she enjoyed for the rest of her life – and to swim in the cold mountain streams. Khalil taught Soraya to ride her own pony, and she would accompany her father whenever he went hunting. As she grew older, she acquired larger mounts and would become an accomplished equestrienne. Khalil's penchant for hunting the gazelles did not meet with Soraya's approval. Watching a gazelle being shot when running away would make her feel sick, but she knew she had to be courageous if she was to merit the title of a Bakhtiari. She remained revolted all her life having to watch an animal, perhaps a sheep, being sacrificed for a party such as a birth or a marriage. Although trying to convince herself she was an Iranian, her subsequent, glamourous lifestyle suggests at heart she was European.

The Tehran Government's restraints on Khalil were something of a paradox as they did not apply to Eva. Reza Shah Pahlavi's pro-German foreign policy had largely been accepted by most Iranians. The British, French and Soviets were perceived as colonialists. The British control of neighbouring countries such as Iraq and India, and the French of Syria and Lebanon, was seen with hostility. The Soviet acquisition of Azerbaijan had not been forgotten. Furthermore, Britain's arrogance of using Indian troops, seen as an inferior race by the Iranians, to secure the oilfields around Abadan during WWI had rubbed salt in the wound. Eva's nationality and the fact that her father had been an important German industrialist unquestionably lessened the personal boundaries imposed on them by the pro-German government.

An Arranged Marriage

During a state visit by Reza Shah Pahlavi to Turkey in 1934, President Mustafa Kemal Atatürk had discussed with the Shah the idea of creating a Muslim bloc of countries to deter future western aggression of the type that had occurred in WWI. Diplomacy between Turkey, Iran, Afghanistan and Iraq, where extensive oilfields had been discovered in 1927, resulted in an alliance being agreed at the Saadabad Palace near Tehran in July 1937. In a private meeting, Atatürk and Reza Shah agreed that the inclusion of Egypt would considerably strengthen the pact and a marriage between the Iranian and Egyptian courts would be beneficial for the long-term future of their dynasties.

Consequently, on 15th March 1939 in Cairo, the Shah's son, Prince Mohammad Reza, aged nineteen, and Princess Fawzieh, aged eighteen, were married. Fawzieh was the daughter of King Fahad I. Her brother, Farouk, would later become the Egyptian King.

The arranged marriage was never going to be a success. Fawzieh was largely educated privately within the bounds of the Royal Palace and had hardly ever ventured beyond its walls. She had been over-protected and was, consequently, parochial and naive. Under-confident with strangers, her shyness gave the impression that she was cold and unapproachable. By contrast, her husband had been declared Crown Prince when aged six and had been prepared to become the second Pahlavi Shah. His twin sister, Ashraf, was ten minutes older. Not until he was married did the public discover that his sister was the eldest. A first-born should always be a boy.

As Crown Prince of Iran, he had accompanied his father on state visits: Iraq, Afghanistan, Turkey and Egypt. When twelve, he was sent to a Swiss boarding school, Le Rosey, in Rolle on Lake Geneva. Today, it is the most expensive boarding school in the world. Alumni include the Aga Khan, King Bedouin of Belgium, and King Juan Carlos of Spain. There, Mohammed Pahlavi was a model student. He became proficient in English, German and French. A gifted sportsman, he excelled at tennis and soccer. After four years, he returned to enter Iran's Army Officers' School in Tehran. He graduated two years later as a sub-lieutenant in his father's former regiment – the Cossack Brigade.

Living under a secular, relatively liberal regime, the Crown Prince, a Shia Muslim, and his wife, Fawzieh, a Sunni, conceived a daughter. Princess Shahnaz was born on 27th October 1940. The unhappy marriage was common knowledge, as the Crown Prince was openly unfaithful, often seen driving around Tehran in one of his expensive sports cars with girlfriends. His dominating, possessive mother, Nimtaj, took to humiliating Princess Fawzieh. Longing to go back to Egypt, she left Tehran as soon as Germany was defeated in WWII. She never returned to Iran, and Mohammed Shah divorced her in November 1948.

4

WWII IN IRAN

A Three-Week Defeat

In June 1941, after the Nazi invasion of the Soviet Union, the USSR and Britain became allies. This had a major impact on Iran, which had declared its neutrality in 1939. However, the Shah's railroads had been designed by German workers who were administering the network. With the German Army steadily advancing through the Soviet Union, an Iranian corridor using the Trans-Iranian Railway was the easiest way to supply the Soviets with goods from Britain and the United States via the Persian Gulf.

U-boat attacks and severe gales made the alternative Barents Sea route to Archangel hazardous. Therefore, Churchill and Stalin agreed to attack Iran to both secure the supply of oil for the Allies and the easier aid-route to the Soviets. The Allies delivered diplomatic notes to the Iranian Prime Minister, Ali Mansur, on 19th July and 17th August 1941. The second of the notes was an ultimatum: expel all German nationals, or take the consequences.

On 25th August 1941, Anglo-Soviet forces jointly invaded Iran in Operation Countenance. Prior to the attack, the RAF dropped leaflets on Iranian cities explaining to the population that their country was not threatened. Rather, it was being liberated from potential Nazi occupation. The Soviets advanced from Azerbaijan to secure Tehran while the British used the Royal Navy to land predominantly Indian and Australian troops in the south to control the AIOC's oilfields around Abadan.

Total control of Iran was achieved in three weeks as the token resistance by outnumbered Iranians to defend their country on two fronts was futile. Atatürk and Reza Shah's Saadabad Pact had proved ineffective. Iran would remain split in two for the duration of the war. The collapse of the Iranian army was embarrassing for the Shah and his son. The Crown Prince's humiliation might explain the inordinate amounts of money he would later spend on military hardware. The Soviets based their headquarters in Tabriz, while in the south the British set up their HQ in Hamadan, a town midway along the strategic road between Tehran and Baghdad. Most German citizens residing in the British sector were deported from Iran to Australia. The vast region of eastern Iran, mostly desert, came under joint Anglo-Soviet control. The main supply route for British and American aid to the USSR was secure for the rest of the war and became known as the Iranian Corridor.

In August 1945, the British began withdrawing peacefully from Iran. However, the Soviets refused to evacuate their troops from the north, using the spurious excuse of security. It took a meeting of the UN Security Council in June 1946, to persuade the Soviets to withdraw from northern Iran back to their Soviet Socialist Republic of Azerbaijan. Hussein Ala, Iran's Foreign Minister, faced Gromyko, who backed down as the USSR at that time didn't have sufficient confidence to confront both the US and the UK. The world's press announced *Persian lion punches Russian bear*. It was the first complaint filed by a country in the UN's history.

However, communist militias were making trouble in northern Iran who wished to be absorbed into the Azerbaijan SSR. In December 1946, the young Shah led a brigade of his Cossack Army to quash resistance. His easy victories permanently ensured the northern boundary with the Azerbaijan.

Although Mrs Mantel's small, private school was allowed to remain open, Soraya lost her German school friends. In order to prepare Soraya for eventually attending the local secondary school, it was essential to employ a private, female tutor to improve Soraya's mastery of Farsi. However, Soraya knew her female teacher's weaknesses. Bent on having her own way, Soraya would climb the trees in their garden, daring her teacher to come and get her down. Progress was, consequently, disappointing. Khalil realised Soraya's charismatic, spirited personality required a different approach.

Reza Shah Deposed

Within a week of the beginning of the August invasion, the Iranian army had effectively collapsed. Most Iranian soldiers fled to the south away from the advancing Soviets.

Reza Shah wanted to have his generals shot, but the Crown Prince pleaded with his father that they should be made to resign. Only the Shah and his son remained in Tehran as the rest of the extended Pahlavi family and their Court fled to Isfahan. Reza Shah surrendered, hoping to negotiate with the allies. However, they immediately insisted all German nationals be handed over. The Shah dallied for several days, allowing many Germans to escape to neutral Turkey. Impatient, the Allies enforced the Shah's abdication on 17th September.

The British initially wanted to restore the Qajar Dynasty because it had assisted British oil interests during WWI. However, there was no suitable Qajar heir to the throne. The most eligible candidate, who lived in Monaco, couldn't even speak Farsi. By default, the Allies agreed that the Crown Prince should replace his father and was inaugurated as the new Shah.

Reza Shah was sent into exile in South Africa, where he died in 1944. Much of the credit for the relatively smooth transition of power from the old Shah to his son was largely due to the efforts of newly appointed Prime Minister Foroughi. He argued strongly that the Allies must retain the Pahlavi dynasty as he believed the Soviets were angling to have Iran become a socialist republic after the war.

On 19th September, Mohammed Pahlavi agreed to help the Allies and a general amnesty was declared. In return, the Soviets agreed to withdraw from Tehran to allow the young Shah remain in the capital supervising a largely impotent government. The Allies' supplies to the Soviets were secure.

Four days after his accession, Mohammed Shah issued an amnesty to all political prisoners who had suffered under his father's regime. The Bakhtiari families resumed their influential positions in southwestern Iranian society. There, they prospered as the Allies' aid arrived through the Persian Gulf to be transported north through their land.

Although lacking self-confidence in his new role, the young Shah coped well with the allied occupation. He successfully hosted the Tehran Conference in 1943 between Churchill, Roosevelt and Stalin at his Marble Palace.

School in Isfahan

Meanwhile, Khalil was insisting Soraya must undertake an Iranian secondary education and become a Shia Muslim. After her first tutor had been a disaster, Khalil employed a retired Imam to come to their house after Soraya had finished Mrs Mantel's school in the afternoon. His role was to teach Soraya the government's secondary-school syllabus in Farsi. Dressed from head to toe in black, he would neither tolerate lack of effort nor fall for Soraya's charms. Soraya admits in her second autobiography that, before he came, she knew nothing of Iran's history, geography, legends or religion. Being able to speak German, Lori and Russian, as well as the play the piano, didn't count at high school. Initially she was bottom of the class. When Soraya, with crocodile tears, grumbled to her father about her tutor, Khalil would tell her that gain meant pain. Determined not to let her father down, she used her linguistic gift to learn by repetition: history, geography, numbers, tables, formulae. She gritted her teeth. Within six months, she caught up with the others of her own age and was able to progress smoothly over the years to the 10th grade. She learnt history from Darius to the Qajar dynasty, literature such as *A Thousand and One Nights*, religion and the foundation of the Shia sect of Islam. Geography – the borders of Iran are Afghanistan, India, Iraq, and Turkey. Arithmetic – if two trains travelling respectively at 40km/h and 60km/h leave two stations 600km apart, how long will it take for them to meet?

Adab High School, a former English missionary school, had been absorbed into the Iranian educational system in 1939. She remembered the grey uniform, the coke stove in the classroom that poisoned the air, homework, exams, no time for going to the cinema, and a photograph in the classroom of the Shah and his beautiful wife, Fawzieh. Like so many teenagers of her generation, she wanted to become a film star like Vivien Leigh. She had fallen for Clark Gable in *Gone with the Wind*. When she told her parents of her ambitions, they were sufficiently savvy to turn her goal back on her. Their reply was that she would have to become fluent in both English and French. To help her improve, Eva suggested she should write her own play in English. Soraya met the challenge, casting herself as a strong-willed Scarlett O'Hara – a princess rescued by Rhett Butler. Set in an imaginary oriental country, she chose to be a resolute, determined, passionate character – attributes she would show in abundance in her future life. Soraya's love of literature was fuelled by Eva, who loved to read detective novels with her in either English or French. Soraya remembered Sherlock Holmes and Hercule Poirot while dreaming of visiting London and Paris.

She cycled alone to school every day. Her young cousin, Goli, told me of remembering Soraya riding furiously as if she had wings. As Goli's mother had been to Adab School, her mother could speak both German and English and had become a close friend of Eva. Each year, they attended Khalil and Eva's home for a Christmas party. The cousin vividly remembers being amazed at the beauty of the Christmas tree, decorated in the German style.

Soraya progressed rapidly through the grades and left, aged fifteen, in 1947 with a distinction on her school leaving certificate. Soraya was competent speaking Farsi, Lori, German, French, English and Russian.

Image Bakhtiari Photo
Soraya with mother, Eva, and brother, Bijan in garden.

5

RETURN TO EUROPE

Schooling in Switzerland

Upset by Germany's defeat in WWII with its consequent devastation, Eva wanted to be near her elderly parents. Berlin had been partitioned after the war between the four Allied powers and although her parents lived in the British sector, Khalil persuaded Eva that Switzerland, rather than Germany, would be a safer place to raise their children.

Khalil successfully applied to join Iran's diplomatic corps. No doubt with the aid of an uncle in Iran's Foreign Ministry, together with his fluency in German, French and English, he easily passed the selection board. After six months' training, he was posted as an assistant to the Iranian ambassador in Switzerland.

In September 1947, Khalil and Eva rented a house in the Wollishofen quarter of Zurich, a predominantly German-speaking district that allowed Eva to rediscover her *joie de vivre*. Whereas Bijan went to the local school, Soraya was sent to a girls' boarding school, La Priantière, in French-speaking Montreux. The school was chosen by her parents in the belief that the college had a strong reputation for disciplining independently minded teenage girls. Eva warned Soraya she would have to keep her nails short and wear her hair in plaits. Eva stressed there was to be no "larking about". How wrong Eva was to be; the school turned out to be something akin to St Trinian's.

The girls, aged between thirteen and twenty, were from the four corners of the world: Argentina, Canada, Indonesia, Russia, and Europe. Educated in French, they were taught decorum, deportment, and etiquette in order to prepare them for becoming eligible young ladies. Useful subjects included haute cuisine, ballroom dancing, the history of art, and French literature – Hugo, Dumas and Molière. Soraya soon discovered, depending on their age, the girls had more or less total freedom. They could go to the cinema, come back late, use nail varnish, wear lipstick, and have high heels. As she gave the illusion of being older than fifteen, she joined a group of older girls. She was in a paradise previously forbidden. However, it didn't last long. Caught going out late one evening by a member of staff, Eva was informed that Soraya had been gated. After pleading with her mother not to tell Khalil, she was given permission to go to the cinema on Saturday afternoons but to be back by six o'clock. There were to be no more coffee bars or clothes shops.

In winter, skiing was taught at the school's chalet in Gstaad. In summer, tennis and swimming were accepted as being suitable for their pupils. Soraya excelled at all sports, particularly skiing.

She had become an attractive teenager with long, raven-black hair and a fine, slim figure. Her emerald-green eyes fascinated all who knew her. Her mysterious beauty made her the centre of attention.

Whenever asked by her parents about her ambition, she had never wavered – she wanted to be an actress. Although not entirely happy with the idea, they realised that she would have to go to a drama college. To be successful in film, it had to be an English college. When sixteen, she moved to a much more scholastic academy, Les Roseaux, in Lausanne, where most lessons were taught in English. There was less culture, more academe. She buckled down to learn Shakespeare, particularly enjoying *Hamlet*, also her father's favourite play. She memorised Keats's poems as well as reading the Brontë sisters and Trollope. After a year, her father congratulated her on her brilliant results. It was her chance to plead to be allowed to go to London.

London, 1950

Khalil realised that the fearless personality Soraya had shown when younger – with boys, animals or strangers – was an independent streak. She wanted to paddle her own canoe. Soraya begged to be allowed to go to London and, cunningly at one point, quoted from Hamlet, *I shall in all my best obey you.* Her father replied immediately, *Tis a loving and fair reply.* She'd won Khalil's agreement to go. Although unhappy about the idea, he relented when discovering that two of his nephews, Goudraz and Malekshah, were both studying English in London. They were accompanied by their mother, Khalil's cousin Shawkat. They were living in a rented apartment near St James's Park. A room was found for Soraya on the same floor and Shawkat agreed to chaperone Soraya. In the summer of 1950, aged eighteen, but with her mother's reluctant blessing, she left to undertake an English language course in preparation to go to a drama school. Eva's concerns were based on her belief that there was considerable resentment against Germans in London where the Nazis' wartime bombing raids had been greatest. Eva need not have fretted, for Soraya's cousins would not let her out of their sight. Shawkat regularly informed Khalil of Soraya's progress. One of the boys always accompanied her whenever she went out to the cinema, window shopping or to college.

During college holidays, she stayed with her parents in Switzerland. On several occasions, suitors from Tehran came to ask Khalil for Soraya's hand in marriage. Accompanied by Khalil and Eva, she would be introduced at dinner to the suitor and his family. Afterwards, she would be questioned privately by her potential fiancé's parents.

Interrogation over, Khalil would ask Soraya what she felt. Allegedly, she would always reply that the boy was very unsuitable and she disliked everything about him.

Trouble for the Shah

Shah Mohammed Pahlavi's divorce from Princess Fawzieh had been confirmed by the Egyptian courts as soon as she left Tehran in 1945. Their daughter, Shahnaz, remained with her father in Iran to be educated at a boarding school in Switzerland. His divorce from Fawzieh was not confirmed in Iran until November 1948.

During these three years, the Shah's mother, Nimtaj, despite knowing her son was a playboy, searched for his next wife. Nimtaj, a secularist like her deceased husband, had been influential in removing the requirement for women to wear the veil in public. She had always insisted on attending civic functions wearing western clothes. Her overriding quest to find her son a suitable young virgin, from a secular, aristocratic family, was proving difficult.

Countless candidates were introduced to the young Shah, or he was shown their photographs, although few were deemed suitable. Nimtaj often saw them as wannabe starlets from inappropriate families. Even the daughter of Hussein Ala, who was to become Prime Minister on two future occasions, was not considered sufficiently suitable.

One of the several Bakhtiaris, who had been held as a political prisoner by Reza Shah but given an amnesty by the young Shah, was Amir Hussein Zafar. He was a son of Sardar Zafar, a senator in the Majlis and a major Bakhtiari clan leader. Amir Zafar and the Shah became lifelong friends. In August, 1950, Amir fell ill. Unannounced, the Shah paid him a visit at Amir's home. While waiting in the drawing room, the Shah began flicking through a photo album on a coffee table. When Amir appeared, the Shah asked about a girl in the family snapshot scrapbook. Amir replied that it was his cousin's daughter. The Shah remarked how attractive she was and that he would like to meet her.

One of Nimtaj's ladies-in-waiting was Forough Zafar, Amir's sister. Amir suggested to his sister that it might be worth mentioning the Shah's interest in Soraya to Nimtaj.

When Forough had an opportunity, she mentioned to Nimtaj that the Shah had seen a photograph of Soraya and had thought she was very pretty. Forough explained Soraya had been well educated in Switzerland and spoke several languages. Furthermore, she was currently in England improving her English. Consequently, Nimtaj asked to see some more photographs of Soraya. Forough contacted Shawkat and asked her to get some photos as soon as possible. It was September 1950.

The Snapshot

Shawkat's son, Goudraz, was an enthusiastic photographer and delighted in taking photos of his cousin. Knowing the photos were to be sent back to his mother's half-sister in the Tehran Court, he used several reels of film before being satisfied. He kept the reason for his zeal from Soraya. On seeing the snaps, the Shah's mother immediately sent her eldest daughter, Princess Shams, to London to investigate Soraya's suitability.

Simultaneously, Khalil was directed by his boss, the ambassador at the Swiss embassy, to present his daughter to Court as soon as possible. Soraya received a letter from her father stressing that there were no strings attached to the invitation and, consequently, he had accepted.

The penny was beginning to drop. Soraya, no fool, pressed Goudraz to tell her what was going on. He admitted the photos were for the

Photo Bakhtiari picture
Soraya about to leave school and go to London

Shah's mother as she was seeking potential candidates for her son's future wife. Neither Soraya nor her cousins were taking this seriously until a few days later when Shawkat, her two sons and Soraya were invited to dine with Princess Shams at Iran's London Embassy.

Paris Interlude

Soraya was initially reluctant to meet Princess Shams because of the Pahlavis' historic antagonism towards the Bakhtiaris, but her natural inquisitiveness got the better of her. On meeting Shams, Soraya was impressed. Shams appeared to be elegant, amiable, and unpretentious. Despite their age difference and background – Shams was thirty-four and married – they hit it off instantly. The following day, they went to the theatre, having spent the afternoon visiting the Victoria and Albert Museum. Shams admitted she knew Soraya had been invited to Court and suggested they spent some time together in Paris, from where they could fly to Rome and meet Soraya's father en route to Tehran.

Before leaving, Princess Shams dispatched a telegram from the London embassy to tell her mother that she need look no further. Described as beautiful, intelligent, and graceful, Shams wrote Soraya would make an ideal wife for her brother. The Shah was shown the photographs, read Shams' telegraph and at once sent a reply for his sister to return to Tehran with Soraya.

Princess Shams and Soraya went to Paris and booked into the Hotel Crillon, on the Place de la Concorde. It was an eye-opener for the eighteen-year-old. They visited the fashion shops of Dior, Balmain and Fath, attended the theatre, and toured the Louvre. Like any other eighteen-year-old, Soraya was flattered by the attention and the euphoria of the high life. They spent long hours in tea rooms and at fashion houses where Shams wanted Soraya to try on everything. Shams' indecision amused Soraya – even irritating her on occasions. Her passion to fit out Soraya with a suitable wardrobe seemed boundless, and she admitted in her first biography of being astounded by everything happening so quickly.

Over four days, she promised that if Soraya married the Shah, then she would give Soraya her full support. However, Shams did warn her that becoming the queen would not be a bed of roses. There would be many unpleasant aspects to it.

Palace Intrigue

Shams tutored Soraya that it was important she knew who was who in the Court. The princess showed photos of the more important members, describing their characteristics and roles, who was dependable and who was not. One by one, Shams covered the Shah's brother and half-brothers, the Shah's mother and her ladies-in waiting, the government cabinet ministers, and the Shah's personal advisers. Shams tutored Soraya on poise, deportment, bowing and curtseying, even accent enunciation. Above all, she warned Soraya against trusting Princess Ashraf, the Shah's twin sister who she described as ambitious and scheming. Shams accused her of usually being the instigator of the Royal Court intrigue, blaming her for the break-up of the Shah's marriage to Fawzieh.

Shams described how her own wish to marry her husband, whose family was not considered socially acceptable, had not been approved by Nimtaj and Ashraf. The pair had pressured the Shah to forbid the wedding, necessitating Shams to elope to Egypt where she married secretly. She and her husband then lived in exile in the USA and only after the birth of their second child did the Shah relent and allow Shams to return to Tehran. However, her husband had to change his name and was not allowed to associate with his own family.

The Shah's half-sister, Fatima, had had a similar experience when she had wished to marry an American, Vincent Hillier, a few months previously. They lived near Paris and the Shah had forbidden them ever to return to Iran. Shams took Soraya to meet them. It was dawning on Soraya that Court feuding was complex and worrying. The antipathy between the two sisters led Soraya to wonder if Shams wanted no more than to gain a victory over Ashraf.

Soraya admitted in her biography that everything became blurred – to the point that she didn't know what to believe. Hearing "do this" and "don't do that" continuously drove her to distraction. She told her father of her concerns when she met him in Rome. Khalil explained that a marriage to the Shah would unite the Pahlavis and the Bakhtiaris to the benefit of both families. However, her father assured Soraya that he would never force her to do anything against her will. He added that he would fund her to go to a drama school, if that was what she desired. Reassured, the following day, they flew to Tehran. Eva's absence in Rome was due to her having prearranged to meet her brother in Cologne, whom she hadn't seen for fifteen years.

6

SORAYA MEETS THE SHAH

Preparation

After a twelve-hour wait at Rome airport, the party took an overnight KLM Lockheed Constellation aircraft to Mehrabad Airport, Tehran. With a flight time of almost twelve hours, they arrived at 10.00am on 8th October 1950. One of Khalil's half-brothers, Assad Bakhtiar, was on the same flight, returning from a holiday. He was unaware of what was happening. However, efforts to keep Soraya's move to Tehran a secret had leaked out. A Roman evening newspaper, published before their departure, speculated that the companion with Princess Shams was a young Iranian, *Soraya Esfandiar, the fiancée of the Shah.*

Khalil and Soraya were greeted at Tehran airport by Khalil's cousin, Forough Zafar. She accompanied Soraya and Khalil to the villa of her brother, Amir Zafar. Forough explained during the journey that it was planned for Soraya to be presented to the Shah the following day. Soraya was exhausted after the long trip, unpacked and asked if she could go to bed. Hardly asleep, a written order arrived from the Shah's mother, Nimtaj. It instructed Soraya and Khalil to attend a small, private dinner party at her home that evening.

'It's not an invitation,' remarked Forough. 'It is an order; we must attend.' Soraya could not have realised this was to be the first command she would receive from Nimtaj, the de facto Head of the Pahlavi household.

Within half an hour, Princess Shams arrived at Amir's villa to prepare Soraya for the evening. Soraya never found out how she arrived so quickly. The afternoon was a flurry; there was no time to linger. First the hairdresser arrived – two hours went by. Then Shams chose which dress to wear from those scattered over the bed. The right jewelry had to be selected – a loose necklace or a choker? The shoes had to match the dress – there were many to choose from. Then, perfume and makeup – Shams insisted only a small amount of lipstick. Finally, a revision lesson on protocol – how to courtesy, very low for the Shah, not so low for the dowager, a reminder of names, and so on. By seven o'clock, Shams and Soraya were being driven to Nimtaj's house, with Khalil and Forough following in a second car. Not wishing to raise Soraya's expectations, Shams warned Soraya that her brother was not particularly handsome. It was in total contradiction to Soraya's memory of the picture of the Shah and Queen Fawzieh that had been in every classroom at Adab School. In Soraya's mind, distrust about Shams' motives grew. The distrust would eventually grow to include all of the Pahlavi family, including the Shah.

Reception

The Royal family received Soraya warmly. For a quarter of an hour, they exchanged small talk, enquiring after her health and that of her relatives. She was the centre of attention, while Khalil was on the sidelines being entertained by Forough and Dr Ayadi, the Shah's personal physician. All present awaited the arrival of the Shah.

By tradition, the Shah arrived five minutes late. When a servant announced His Majesty's arrival, everyone stood to attention. The Shah, dressed in the uniform of a general, embraced his mother. His sisters and brother bowed. Soraya curtsied when presented to him.

Instantly, Soraya was spellbound by his entrance. She admits in both her autobiographies that she was mesmerized. She thought he was tall, well built, imposing in his uniform, handsome and gregarious. For Soraya, it was love at first sight.

In reality, he wasn't tall and permanently wore elevated shoes. He was obsessed by height and stature, probably because his father was well-over six feet. His height was probably no more than 5ft 7in, two inches taller than Soraya who was 5ft 5in. A photograph of him standing next to Prince Philip when he visited London shows him at least 4 inches lower than the Prince, who was 6 feet tall.

At the dinner table, against strict etiquette, the Shah asked Soraya to sit next to him. She claimed in her biographies they clicked immediately. Soraya and the Shah, having both been educated in Switzerland, talked non-stop about the country around Montreux and Lausanne. He asked about her likes and dislikes: art, literature and sport. They discovered their love for horses and skiing.

Soraya thought she was being carefully watched by the rest of the Pahlavi family. Their meaningful glances and whispers were summing her up, and she felt they were hoping she would make a faux pas.

After dinner they played a game where everyone took a turn, going around the room, to name a geographical feature beginning with a particular letter: Alaska, Australia, Amazon, etc. If someone couldn't think of an answer, they dropped out until there was a winner. Soraya sensed the family was trying to test her general knowledge.

The party ended around eleven o'clock and Soraya left with her father and Forough. However, at 2.00am, the Shah telephoned Khalil. It had taken the Shah less than six hours from meeting Soraya to make a decision. He asked Khalil for his daughter's hand and wanted to know if she would accept.

Khalil woke Soraya with the news, pointing out that if she accepted, there could be no going back. But he added that if she refused, he would allow her to travel to Hollywood. Soraya's answer was an immediate, 'Yes'. Smitten by the Shah, she was in love for the first time.

Soraya admitted she had felt a flow of tenderness from his first glance, which had captivated her. Flattered by his impatience to ask her father for her hand and being chosen from a simple snapshot left her on cloud nine.

Later that morning, the daily newspapers in Iran were showing the photo that Goudraz had taken on their front pages with the heading, *Our New Queen – Soraya Esfandiar*. The engagement was announced on State radio. The next day, the Shah visited Soraya at Amir Zafar's villa. It was 11th of October 1950. Soraya, aged eighteen years and four months, was destined to become Empress of Iran.

A few days later, an official function was organised at the Imperial Palace for the press, radio and newsreels. Soraya, wearing a 22 carat-solitaire ring, was the centre of attraction. Afterwards, a ball was held. When Shams saw the dress Soraya was intending to wear and had bought in Paris, Shams declared it unsuitable. It was unthinkable for the future queen to be seen with uncovered arms in a sleeveless dress. Within an hour, a seamstress arrived, took the dress away, and a short time later returned it with wide, matching, three-quarter length sleeves.

During the evening, the Shah whispered in Soraya's ear that he wished to show her his favourite room in the marble palace. In an adjoining room, he showed her the library – with marble, ivory and gold panels, full of ancient texts and books. She was studying the rare first editions when she felt one of his arms around her shoulder and the other around her waist. In her biography, Soraya admits to taking fright and rushing back to the ballroom, leaving a disappointed Shah with a crestfallen look.

Courtship and Doubt

The marriage was set for 27th December 1950. Soraya's parents rented a spacious villa in Tehran for themselves, Soraya and Bijan. However, Soraya discovered that Eva had doubts. Although happy for her daughter, she expressed her concern that the duties awaiting Soraya would be overwhelming for one so young. Soraya's reply to her mother was along the lines that she had also married young. However, Eva had the last word, 'I didn't take on the duties of an Empress'.

In the ensuing weeks, the Shah and his fiancée saw one another almost daily; Aunt Forough acted as chaperone. Lunches with the Shah's brothers and sisters helped to get to know his family; they went well. However, visits to meet the Shah's mother tended to be difficult. Soraya sensed the dowager had not recovered from the fact that her husband had gone into exile in 1941 with another woman and hid her feelings towards her children's spouses, soon to include Soraya.

Whenever the couple could, they went riding in the southern foothills of the Alborz Mountains at Shemiran, north of Tehran. They played tennis on an indoor court, or went flying together with the Shah at the controls of his private aircraft – often to have a picnic at the Ramsar Palace on the edge of the Caspian Sea. It offered privacy with its garden of orange and pine trees. Away from the Court followers and their chaperones, Soraya claimed their love blossomed.

As Soraya began to know him better, she realised her fiancé was essentially a reserved man – shy with those he didn't know. His responsibilities restricted him from expressing his feelings. Only his dark eyes reflected his feelings for her. Soraya excused his apparent diffidence by his unhappy upbringing – a doomed arranged marriage, and an authoritarian father who demanded a military childhood with no friends of his own. She was also beginning to appreciate how much influence his overbearing mother had on her under-confident, insecure son.

Nonetheless, Mohammed Shah would talk enthusiastically of his father's achievements. 'He did more for Iran in ten years than the whole of the Qajar Dynasty in 200 years. He constructed roads, built the railway to connect the Caspian to the Persian Gulf, built hospitals in the major cities, sent students abroad to study, and imposed a code of civil law.'

Soraya would listen but had to bite her tongue. She knew his father had decimated clans, including the Bakhtiaris, stolen their property and murdered hundreds of political opponents.

If it wasn't occurring to Soraya, it must have been to her parents, that her love for the Shah was simply a teenager's crush. They had noticed the Shah didn't have a sense of humour – an essential quality for a successful relationship like their own. Accustomed to compliments from his courtiers, he hated criticism. The tiniest rebuke could send him into a fit of pique, which was frightening. Only Ashraf, his twin sister, would stand her ground and quarrel with him.

Soraya tried her best to keep out of such situations. However, one day the Shah began interrogating her.

'What does marriage mean to you?'

She wondered if this was some sort of a test. She thought of her parents – being close, sharing everything, and having children.

'It's being faithful and loyal.'

'What else?'

'Being happy together?'

'What else?'

'I don't know, helping each other?'

'What else?'

The aggressive questions continued until Soraya turned away weeping. The Shah apologised.

A day later, at Ashraf's house for dinner, Ashraf teased her brother that Soraya was too young for him – she being eighteen while he was almost thirty-one. He stiffened visibly and replied, as if Soraya wasn't there, 'In Iran, Empresses have to grow up quickly. With the life ahead of her, she will be obliged to forget her youth.'

It must have dawned on Soraya that her marriage was not going to be peaches and cream. In her biography, she resolved that she would do everything she could to be worthy of her husband.

The couple inspected several Royal palaces in Tehran for their future home. Soraya chose a modest palace on Avenue Pasteur, known as the Echtessassi, ironically the Shah's personal home. However, it badly needed a woman's touch. The sofas were old and shabby, the rooms dull with the curtains faded. When Soraya pointed out it lacked a suitable ambience, the Shah was surprised but agreed to its frugal redecoration. Austerity was the name of the game. One third of the population was unemployed; children wandered the streets with rickets looking for food while the AIOC ferreted away 90% of Iran's oil profits. The Shah made it clear that their wedding was not going to be an ostentatious affair. The towns and villages that would normally organise their own celebrations were being instructed that the money was instead to be earmarked for charity.

On formal occasions, Soraya was frequently chaperoned by Shams who never ceased to give advice, tell her the rules, warn her off people she was to meet, and cast suspicions on those who were unreliable. The harassment left Soraya exhausted and compounded her qualms about the difficulty of the duties that lay ahead when she would be married into what appeared to be a dysfunctional, back-biting family.

Postponement of Wedding

On the 26th October, Soraya returned shivering with a fever from a ride in the Alborz Mountains. Satisfied her daughter had something more serious than a chill, and believing European doctors were better qualified than Iranian ones, Eva found a German doctor to examine her. However, at the Shah's insistence, Dr Ayadi, his personal physician, correctly diagnosed typhoid, as hundreds of other cases had recently broken out in Tehran. He ordered a strict diet and prescribed a variant of streptomycin, called aureomycin. It was an antibiotic discovered in 1948 whose side effects were still unknown.

The Shah visited her every day with presents such as flowers, jewels, and chocolates. A nurse, trained in the United States, was put at Dr Ayadi's disposal. The Shah had a radio installed by her bedside, although Soraya admitted in her biography that she hadn't the inclination to listen to music. Nonetheless, his attentive and sensitive manner bowled her over – his weaknesses were forgotten. However, when he told her that he had had typhoid when aged seven and in a dream had met Ali, Mohammed's son-in-law, then recovered next day, Soraya wrote that his religion worried her. Later, she would discover that he had commanded Imams to say prayers for her recovery in all Iranian mosques. She began wondering if the Shah believed he was elected by God, why did he rarely attend the mosque?

December 27th had been set for their wedding. However, her fever had not abated by mid-November. Her weight was barely six stone and her temperature was frequently as high as 41°C. The Shah, worried and impatient, took advice from Dr Ayadi. The wedding had to be postponed until 1951.

Staying in bed did not suit Soraya's lively temperament. Her frustrations were made worse by both Shams and Ashraf visiting regularly. Each would try to outdo the other. Ashraf made great play of protecting her younger twin brother or brag about meeting President Truman at the White House or Stalin at the Kremlin. Rumours had begun to circulate at Court that Ashraf had poisoned Soraya with a concoction of salmonella germs as she did not wish to lose her influence with her brother. Considering the typhoid epidemic was spreading all over Tehran, the accusation was absurd.

The two princesses' comings and goings annoyed Dr Ayadi; they were doing more harm than good. He insisted that their visits were not to be longer than thirty minutes; a policy he and Soraya's Aunt Forough monitored assiduously.

The Shah's mother, Nimtaj, visited her only once, giving Soraya a pretty broach – a parrot with a pearl and an emerald. Years later, Soraya discovered that it hadn't belonged to Nimtaj, but the Shah had asked his mother to give it to Soraya. It was a small incident but sowed another seed of doubt in her mind that it was Nimtaj who ruled the roost, not the Shah.

With the New Year approaching, the Shah's personal Imam, Imam Jumeh, pointed out that the marriage would have to take place before 13th February, when two consecutive months of *Jumada* would begin. The months are the period of mourning for the death of, firstly, Fatima – the Prophet Mohammed's daughter – and, secondly, the death of Abu Bakr – the father-in-law of Mohammed and first Caliph.

The Shah was spending ever more time at Soraya's bedside with Dr Ayadi in attendance. Soraya's condition was torturing the Shah. Soraya saw him gradually becoming frantic. With Soraya listening in bed, he asked Ayadi if she should be given more vitamins or how could he ensure she will get through the marriage ceremony to take place on Monday, 12th February 1951. Soraya felt guilty, as if her illness was her fault. Her fate had been decided; she had to be fit whatever the cost.

7

THE WEDDING OF THE DECADE

From Soraya's Autobiography: *Le Palais des Solitude*
Wedding Day and the Christian Dior Dress

The Dress

Soraya remained convalescing in bed until a week before the wedding. By then Dr Ayadi had insisted that only he, Forough, the Shah, and Soraya's parents could attend her bedside. A strict diet, prepared under stringent hygienic conditions, was enforced – no chocolates, cakes or pastries. Christian Dior's wedding gown arrived from Paris three days before the ceremony. Adjustments had been made in Paris on one of Nimtaj's younger ladies-in-waiting. It fitted Soraya perfectly. The dress was made of tulle and thirty yards of silver brocade. The train was ten feet long, weighed about fifty pounds, and was studded with 6,000 diamonds and countless sequins. Soraya claimed in her second biography that the diamonds were glass, as the Shah had insisted on economy. However, there is considerable doubt about this claim as all other references to the gown said they were diamonds. When the dress was auctioned after her death, it fetched $1.2 million, suggesting the stones were genuine. The neckline was trimmed with white mink and the hem with over 1,000 marabou feathers.

She donned a diamond tiara, along with an emerald necklace and several emerald bracelets, all chosen to match her green eyes. These jewels were borrowed from the government and were returned after the ceremony. The sleeves of the dress were three-quarter-length and her gloves were white silk. The Shah had given her a white mink, three-quarter-length coat to keep her warm on the way to the palace.

Panic

At her parents' rented villa, while Eva and the ladies-in-waiting bustled around preparing Soraya's dress, checking for the umpteenth time her hair or make-up, Dr Ayadi handed her two pills. Without explaining what they were, he told her to take them, as they would regularise her heart. He also handed her a pair of long, knee-length, white, woollen socks. He explained it was essential that she kept her feet warm, adding that they would not be seen under her dress. Lastly, he slipped a small bottle of smelling salts into the pocket of her mink coat in case she felt faint.

He told her that she was still frail and must keep warm at all costs. If she felt unwell at any time, he assured her that he would be close at hand. His concern for her health confirmed Soraya's growing belief that the doctor was one of a few within the Court whom she could trust genuinely.

The phone had been ringing continuously during the disarray. Finally, someone found time to answer it. It was the Palace wanting to know who had been chosen to accompany Soraya to the ceremony. Much frenzied discussion then took place. Protocol demanded it should be the Mayor of Tehran, as his presence was essential to conduct the civilian part of the ceremony. Eva expected it to be Khalil. At the Palace, Shams won the day. She argued that she had found Soraya, befriended her, and coached her in matters of the Royal Court.

Towards four o'clock, a heated limousine arrived at her parents' villa, accompanied by a troop of lancers. Snow was falling, blanketing the branches of the trees. Window panes were covered with frost. It was one of the coldest days ever recorded in Tehran.

Shams entered the Bakhtiaris' villa to escort Soraya to the Marble Palace. The lancers struggled to keep the horses under control in the snow, while the breath from their nostrils steamed. A further holdup occurred – the ladies-in-waiting struggled to get Soraya's train into the back of the car as it became muddled with Shams' dress, which Soraya later described it as *a veritable parachute of organdie.*

Travelling through the snow-covered streets, the crowds cheered and waved. In the front of the limousine, the Lord Mayor sat next to the chauffeur. They arrived at the entrance to the Golestan Palace;

today it has world heritage status. The group of palaces, halls and gardens were once surrounded by a high wall, forming the Qajar Dynasty's citadel. Yet another holdup then occurred. At the foot of the steps, four small bridesmaids were waiting in the cold for Soraya to arrive. When they went to help Soraya out of the car, they discovered they couldn't lift her train – it was too heavy. They had to wait shivering in the cold while the ladies-in-waiting arrived in the following car to help. Only then could Soraya proceed with the six train-bearers on her five-minute journey up the one-hundred steps to the Hall of Mirrors. The staircase was lined with soldiers of the Imperial Guard, standing rigidly to attention. Despite the weight of her dress making progress difficult, Soraya pulled her shoulders back, held her head high and looked straight ahead. The last words of Khalil, before leaving their villa, were ringing in her ears, 'Remember you are a Bakhtiari.'

Marriage Ceremony

The Hall of Mirrors was decorated with flowers flown in from Holland: twelve hundred branches of lilac, one thousand red carnations, two hundred Japanese Cherry trees, two hundred orchids, and countless tulips – all a gift from Queen Juliana.

The Golestan Palace had no heating, but oil stoves had been installed throughout to keep the guests warm. However, no one had anticipated Soraya having difficulty with the weight of her ten-foot train. As she entered the Hall of Mirrors, the Shah approached wearing the dark-blue uniform of a Field Marshal. His golden epaulettes, rank braids, emperor's sash and medals gleamed. They met in the middle. They held hands while those present either bowed or curtsied. Walking in silence, they proceeded slowly to an anteroom where the formal ceremony was to be conducted by Imam Jumeh. Like the Shah and

Soraya, Imam Jumeh had been educated in Switzerland. He would later become a trusted confident of Soraya.

Apart from the four bridesmaids and the ladies-in-waiting, only present in the anteroom were the Shah's immediate family, Soraya's parents, and the Aga Khan, the Head of the Ismailism sect of Shiism who was the Shah's best man with his wife, the Begum Khan. Soraya and the Shah sat on their thrones opposite a large gold-framed mirror. Persian tradition decreed that couples, once married, should see their spouse for the first time in a mirror.

The Shah, without looking at her, then handed Soraya a crystal cup full of sugar. She passed it to her mother-in-law standing behind them. Nimtaj sprinkled it over their heads, saying, 'May your union be sweet – your thoughts sugared.'

The Koran was placed on Soraya's lap and Imam Jumeh began reciting lengthy passages in Farsi. Her head was in a spin as the recital seemed to last for ever. He finished by asking questions.

'Do you give me the right to conduct this marriage?'

Soraya replied in Farsi, '*Balé.*'

'Do you take Mohammad Reza for your husband?'

'*Balé.*'

The Shah was asked the same questions.

The Imam then declared Soraya, daughter of Khalil, to be the lawful bride of Mohammad Reza. He further declared Mohammed Reza Pahlavi to be the lawful husband of Soraya Esfandiar-Bakhtiar. The couple then looked at each other in the mirror while the Shah placed the wedding ring on Soraya's finger.

The Lord Mayor placed the formal documents in front of them to be signed in the civil part of the ceremony. With immaculate timing, a 21-gun salute was fired outside announcing that the Shah had a new wife.

To conclude the ceremony, according to custom, a lady-in-waiting was to pour a number of small gold coins over the couple.

However, Nimtaj decided to undertake the task. Unknowingly for Soraya, it was a bad omen, for the bearer of the coins was supposed to be happily married and, therefore, was passing on the harmony in her life to the new couple. It was certainly not the job for a bitter widow.

Unknowingly, Soraya had not only married her husband, but also his abnormal, unpleasant, and irrational family.

Reception

The couple returned from the marriage chamber to the Hall of Mirrors and welcomed the diplomats from the various embassies with which Iran had relations. Governments had been asked not to give presents. Rather, they had been requested to donate to Soraya's favourite charity for the poor children of Iran. Nonetheless, gifts abounded. Stalin, not a lover of blue blood but knowing Eva had been born in the Soviet Union, had sent a desk inlaid with black diamonds. President Truman donated a large, five-foot Steuben glass vase. King George VI gave a set of sliver candlesticks. President Figl of Austria delivered a Steinbeck grand piano. However, the AIOC gave half a million pounds sterling to build a new children's hospital.

There was much handshaking, introductions, polite conversations, smiling and standing. Soraya began to feel faint and short of breath. The weight of the train was still dragging behind her. The Shah, quick to notice her discomfort, nodded to Dr Ayadi. They excused themselves, returning to the wedding chamber. Another pick-me-up was prescribed, along with the smelling salts, while a lady-in-waiting was ordered by the Shah to cut material from her train. Overall, ten yards of rustling tulle, silver brocade and organza were removed. With her dress feeling lighter, she quickly recovered. She found she could move. In her own words, *I felt I was floating.*

They returned to the hall and completed the diplomatic necessities. No one seemed to notice the alterations to her wedding dress. The senior foreign ambassador, from the Soviet Union, congratulated the couple on behalf of the *corps diplomatique*.

The party then moved to another hall within the Golestan Palace for the banquet where three hundred guests sat. All stood as the bridal pair took their place at the top-table. The centrepiece was a five-foot wedding cake. The six-course menu included Caspian caviar, lobster thermidor with crab and avocado, pheasant with asparagus, ice creams, and fresh fruit. Between each course came the speeches, each with a champagne toast. Finally, the couple moved to the Great Ballroom to meet some of the 1,600 guests from all over the world who had not been invited to the wedding banquet. In the reception room stood the famous Peacock Throne, studded with diamonds. The Tehran Symphony Orchestra played background music, including works by Beethoven, Soraya's favourite composer. The couple walked side by side holding hands between the throng, who parted in front of them. Occasionally, they stopped to talk to those guests known to the Shah.

A continuous buffet had been laid out at one end of the reception area. Soraya described feeling lightheaded. Worried she might faint but with a fixed smile for everyone, she managed to cope. When many guests went outside to watch the firework display, she remained resting on the throne with the Shah. Thousands of flowers had been planted in the illuminated gardens to create a fairy-tale wonderland. The frozen lake had underwater lights that added to the illusion that spring had arrived early. An equestrian circus brought from Rome further entertained the guests.

The ball lasted until midnight, when Soraya and her husband retired to their new home, the Echtessassi Palace. The entire route was massed with cheering men, women and children who had waited in the freezing conditions to catch a glimpse of their new empress.

Mounting Crisis

Their first two days were spent in their new home, where they discussed the country's problems with the Aga Khan and his wife. A crisis had been mounting for almost a year, the root cause being the AIOC's distribution of its profits. With his extensive, worldwide contacts, the Aga Khan's advice was considered invaluable.

Afterwards, instead of honeymooning in Capri, the crisis demanded they remained near Tehran. In the Shah's private aircraft, they flew to the Shah's small palace at Ramsar on the Caspian Sea. Soraya regained her strength as they spent time together, despite courtiers and ministers arriving daily to update the Shah on developments. Apart from the squabbling over oil with Britain and the United states, there was the ongoing three-way confrontation with the Mosaddeq nationalists, the Tudeh Communist Party and Ayatollah Kashani who retained links with the terrorist brotherhood – the Fedayeen. Each day, the Shah spent endless hours with his ministers, usually emerging, in Soraya's words – *with furrows lining his forehead.* The Shah was trying to hide from Soraya his worst fears for the future.

Whenever possible, their time together was, according to Soraya, passionate, sensitive, and full of intense shared happiness. She slowly recovered from her illness but remained indoors to keep warm whenever the Shah went riding.

After three weeks, state matters demanded the Shah returned to Tehran. Their honeymoon, far from ideal, was over.

8

POLITICAL PROBLEMS

Mosaddeq and the Nationalists

Born into a branch of the Bakhtiari family in June 1882, Mohammed Mosaddeq was distantly related to one of the Qajar Shahs through his mother. Educated at the University of the Sorbonne in Paris, Mosaddeq gained a Master's degree in International Law in 1911. He subsequently gained a PhD from the University of Neufchatel in Switzerland before teaching at the Tehran School of Political Science.

Mosaddeq had endured the Anglo-Russian occupation of Persia during WWI that gave the Allies their source of oil. When the war finished, both the neutral Soviet government and the British initially agreed to withdraw their troops – the Soviets back to the Caucuses, and the British into Iraq that they controlled. However, the British Foreign Secretary, Lord Curzon, saw an opportunity for Britain to become the dominant power in the region. In 1919, he proposed an Anglo-Persian Agreement that would guarantee exclusive rights for British oil extraction in the southern oil fields. In exchange, Britain would equip and train the Persian Army, offer loans for approved projects, and help build roads. The scheme was heavily criticised by the USA, France and the Soviets who saw the treaty as an act of British colonialism. The USSR fortified their Iranian boundary to protect their interests in the oilfields around Baku. They made it clear to the British that the Azerbaijan province was to become permanently a Soviet Socialist Republic.

Mosaddeq led a protest to the proposed 1919 agreement and was elected to the Iranian Parliament, the Majlis, in order to organise widespread opposition. With the country in total chaos, the Majlis signed a peace treaty with the Soviets in February 1921, agreeing to recognise the Soviet State of Azerbaijan. Simultaneously, they rejected the Anglo-British Agreement but accepted the status quo contract with the APOC.

By April 1921, Reza Khan, having agreed the Soviet treaty, became both the Head of the Army and Minister of War. In October 1923, he became Prime Minister. In 1925, the supporters of Reza Khan in the Majlis proposed legislation to dissolve the Qajar dynasty that had ruled since 1742 and appoint Reza as the new Shah. Mosaddeq voted against the proposal, arguing it was against the constitution. He praised Reza Khan's achievements but pleaded with him to remain as prime minister. On 12th December 1925, the Majlis deposed Ahmad Shah Qajar, who went into exile in France, and declared Reza Shah Pahlavi as the new Shah. Mosaddeq resigned from the Majlis on 11th February 1926 in protest. It made him a marked man by the Pahlavi clique even though he retired from active politics and returned to teaching.

Mosaddeq Post-WWII

As WWII was approaching its finale, in March 1944, Mosaddeq was re-elected to parliament and became the leader of a new party – the Iranian National Front. Its long-term aim was to nationalize the Anglo-Iranian Oil Company and reduce the Shah to a constitutional monarch. The party's slogan was: "The Shah should hold royal office, but not govern". The country, having been run jointly by the British and the Soviets during the war, had effectively made the Majlis a rubber-stamp organization headed by the young Shah. When the war finished, Mosaddeq was determined to restore the Majlis' power. He began preparing a constitutional reform act with the Shah as a constitutional monarch.

After the British and Soviet withdrawal at the end of the war, the post-war period in Iran became progressively more and more unstable. For example, between 1946 and 1951 there were no fewer than seven prime ministers of the Majlis, some serving twice. In 1947, when the Mosaddeq electoral-reform bill failed to pass through Majlis, Mosaddeq again resigned from parliament.

Glad that Mosaddeq had left the Majlis, the Shah tried to appease the remaining Nationalists. In 1948, the Shah appointed Asadollah Alam as Minister of Agriculture to draw up a plan: "The Imperial Redistribution of Agricultural Land". The Shah's idea was to give one million hectares of his land to set up cooperative farms along the line of those in the Soviet Union. Although not in parliament, Mosaddeq smelt a rat. There was a hidden snag. An independent bank would collect the rent paid by the farmers and would reinvest the money. However, the principal shareholder of the bank was the Shah. Mosaddeq had seen through the scheme that effectively relieved the Shah of the cost of looking after his own land, but at the same time gave him an income. The Shah's attempt to bolster his wealth was revealed. Mosaddeq disclosed the plan to friends in the Majlis where opposition was soon total. The Shah lost face, making Mosaddeq a marked man by both Pahlavi and Asadollah Alam. The fiasco gave the members of the National Front a confidence boost to reintroduce their bill on reorganizing the oil industry and the Shah's reduced role.

The National Front's push to nationalize the oil industry gained momentum. In June 1950, seeing the possible consequences, the

British Foreign Office persuaded the Shah that Ali Razmara, an army general trained at the military academy at St Cyr in France, would be a better man to control Iran than the government of Ali Mansur. Without questioning the British motives, the naive Shah appointed Razmara prime minister on 26th June. However, the reason for the British duplicity soon became apparent – control of the AIOC. In desperation, the Shah and Asadollah Ala began ratcheting up their plot to defeat Mosaddeq and the National Front once and for all. Seeing trouble brewing in the Majlis, Mosaddeq got himself re-elected to parliament with the intention of wrecking the British plans.

The Tudeh and the Fedayeen

Prime Minister Razmara began well, proposing a seven-year plan for the decentralization of government and calling for the setting up of regional councils to run affairs such as health, education and agriculture. In order for the decentralization changes to be implemented, he proposed to make 100,000 civil servants redundant. His actions upset the powerful landowners, the merchants, the communist Tudeh Party, the extreme Islamist Fedayeen, and the nationalists. Razmara had to go.

Razmara also agreed a draft contract with the British AIOC and the US Standard Oil Company to allow them control Iran's oil industry. When the details were announced in the Majlis, all hell broke loose. The terms were worse than those agreed by US Standard Oil with Venezuela and Saudi Arabia. To prevent a rebellion, Razmara asked the AIOC to allow Iranian auditors to review the company's finances and train Iranians for managerial jobs. The British refused. Their intransigence was eventually to prove a disaster. The Shah, allowing for them to be conned by the British FO and the AIOC, stretched the Majlis' patience beyond its limit.

From 1941 to 1950, the Shah's inability to control his government's agenda had seen the standard of living of the people decline. Most lived in poverty and squalor. Although well intentioned, the Shah was too ready to compromise. By trying to please everyone – the Majlis, the clergy, the bazaars and the intelligentsia – he ended up satisfying no one. By marrying Soraya in February 1951, some weight would be taken off his shoulders, but enjoyment with his teenage bride would not last long. Lying ahead would be more political problems, his overbearing mother interfering with his marriage, and the need to produce an heir.

Assassination

On Wednesday, 7th March 1951, Razmara went to a mosque for a memorial service. The police opened a corridor through the crowds for him. A nearby assassin fired three quick shots, fatally wounding the Prime Minister. Khalil Tahmassebi, a member of the Fedayeen, was arrested at the scene. At a public demonstration the following day, the Fedayeen distributed leaflets threatening to assassinate the Shah, government officials, and any Majlis member who opposed the nationalization of the AIOC if the assassin was not freed.

Trying to appease the rioters, the Shah panicked and appointed Hussein Ala to replace Razmara. Everyone knew his appointment was merely a stopgap. With Ala only a few weeks in office, a proposal was made by Mosaddeq in the Majlis:

To secure the well-being of the Persian people, it is resolved that the country's entire oil industry be nationalized. All petroleum production will henceforth be managed by the Iranian Government.

No one in the Majlis voted against the bill. Facing impossible odds,

Hussein Ala resigned on 27th April 1951 and the next day Mosaddeq was elected democratically to become Prime Minister by seventy-nine votes to six. The Shah had no alternative but to accept Mosaddeq as his new Prime Minister. A week later, the Oil Nationalization Act came into force and the AIOC's properties were expropriated.

With Soraya as Empress for less than three months, a severe blow had been dealt to the Shah, who was teetering on the brink of losing his sovereignty.

9

THE INDECISIVE SHAH

Court Intrigue

Soraya was beginning to believe her husband's shyness was a weakness that was being exploited by those around him for their own ends. Indecisiveness, uncertainty, and procrastination summed up his character perfectly. Whenever he was faced with a problem, he conferred with advisers whose recommendations would invariably mean change from the status quo. In the fifteen years that his father had been Shah from 1926 to 1941, there had only been six prime ministers, but in the ten years of Mohammed Pahlavi's reign to April 1951, there had been fifteen changes.

Morteza Yazdan-Panah

The one close, trustworthy adviser to Mohammed Shah Pahlavi was General Yazdan-Panah. He had served the Shah's father loyally since 1926. The inexperienced Mohammed Shah appointed him Head of the Imperial Court when he succeeded the throne in 1941. Simultaneously, the General's Russian-born wife, Leyla, became the senior lady-in-waiting to Queen Fawzieh. Both the Yazdan-Panahs were to remain in their posts during the reigns of Soraya and the Shah's third wife, Farah: the general until his death in 1970 and Leyla until the Shah's overthrow in 1979. The general's relationship with the Shah could be described as that of a surrogate uncle.

Morteza Yazdan-Panah had been born in Tehran in 1884. In 1907, he attended the Cossack Cadet School where he learned Russian and by 1921 had risen to Brigadier. Always loyal to Reza Khan, he was promoted to Major General and Chief Inspector of the Army in 1928. Mohammad Shah further promoted him to Lieutenant General in 1942, making him Minister of War, as well as Head of the Imperial Court.

Panah would give his advice when asked but would not try to assert his opinion. He was always there for the Shah – consistently reliable for twenty-nine years until he died. He was responsible for arranging the coronation of Queen Farah – generally agreed to have been a great success, not over-the-top like later Pahlavi celebrations, such as the 2,500[th] celebration of Persia's history.

The General's son was married to one of my contacts, Soraya's cousin, for twelve years. She remembers the General was not averse to letting slip confidences. He often told his wife that the Shah was afraid of his own shadow. Regularly, when accompanying the Shah to open a new public utility, such as a hospital, or a school, the Shah would insist on telling everyone that it was his idea. However, the accompanying members of Court knew the ideas were always someone else's.

The Shah's Psychological Pillars

In his book, *The Pride and the Fall: Iran, 1974-79*, Sir Anthony Parsons, a former British Ambassador to Iran, wrote that the Shah relied on three psychological pillars above all the other advisers in his

Court. Parsons claims that they manipulated the Shah to their own ends rather than to the benefit of his country.

Ernest Peron

Reluctant to dismiss ministers face to face, the Shah would prefer to delegate the unpleasant task to one of his minions. Most unpopular within the Court was Ernest Peron. The Shah had befriended him when at Le Rosey School, where he had been a servant. Peron had supposedly introduced the Shah to French literature. The young Mohammed Pahlavi had brought him back to Iran as a companion when returning permanently from Switzerland. His father, Reza Shah, did not approve, thinking their relationship may be homosexual. It must be stressed there is no evidence to substantiate this. However, Soraya, in her second autobiography, made no bones about it. She called him *"a homosexual who detested all women"*. Describing him as ugly, ungainly, and with a revolting mouth, Soraya clearly hated him. Peron would slander Shams and Ashraf behind their backs. Even the Shah's mother was not beyond his smears.

Reza Shah, after his son's pleading for Peron to stay, eventually relented and allowed Peron to stay at Ramsar, but he was forbidden to enter Tehran. After marrying Princess Fawzieh in 1939, Mohammed Pahlavi had to curtail his visits to Peron at Ramsar. Their strange friendship strained the relationship between the crown prince and his young wife. The Court believed Peron was very influential in hastening the young couple's divorce. After Reza Shah's exile in 1941, Mohammed Reza allowed Peron to move into the Tehran Court. Soraya's cousin wrote to me that the young Shah *"was seemingly fascinated by him"*. She added that the Shah would shut himself in his room with Peron, supposedly to discuss affairs of State or to gather gossip that he'd gleaned from the bazaar.

Soraya claimed Peron told her that he knew of intimate bedroom secrets between her and the Shah while he made an advance towards her. She immediately banned him from her presence, describing Peron as *"a limping devil who spread his poison around the palace".*

Nevertheless, Peron remained the Shah's closest confident, holding their daily private meetings until Peron died in 1960.

No one knew exactly what Peron did or why he had a Svengali-like hold over the Shah. Proclaiming to be a philosopher, Peron is described by Sir Anthony Parsons as *"the most dangerous of the Shah's three psychological pillars".*

Asadollah Alam

Asadollah Alam was born on 24th July 1919 in Birjand, a small city in the east of Persia, a few months before the birth of Mohammed Pahlavi and his twin sister. Alam's heritage was an old, powerful, aristocratic family who were governors of the Birjand region. Alam's father was Amir Ibrahim Alam, distantly related to and a strong supporter of Reza Shah Pahlavi, for whom he had been Minister of Telecommunications.

In 1937, Reza Shah Pahlavi had sought to legitimise his dynasty by integrating powerful, trusted families with arranged marriages.

Firstly, he began arranging for his daughter, Princess Shams, aged twenty-one, to marry Sahib Qavam, the son of Qavam al-Molk who was the head of the most powerful family in the rich, southern province of Pars. Historically, Qavam al-Molk was one of the strongest supporters of Reza Shah.

Secondly, he planned for Asadollah Alam to marry Qavam al-Molk's daughter, Malektaj. Thereby, Asadollah Alam would become Princess Shams' brother-in-law.

Finally, he told his eighteen-year-old daughter, Princess Ashraf, that she was to marry Fereydoun Djam, the son of the prime minister.

However, on the evening before the dual weddings, Shams asked her father to allow her to swap partners, because she preferred Djam. The Shah agreed. So at the eleventh hour, Ashraf had to marry the man who was supposed to be her sister's husband. The sudden change not only hurt Ashraf, but scarred her personality for the rest of her life. Thereafter, the relationship between the two sisters was one of bitter antagonism.

Alam had become the main landowner of the Birjand region after his father's death in 1948. Over several years, he slowly began to distribute his holdings to the peasants, insisting that they should eat as well as his family. Alam's policy met with the approval of the young Shah. As a result, the Shah made Asadollah Minister of Agriculture to implement the Imperial Redistribution of Agricultural Land policy. He also became a close personal adviser to the Shah. The plan was not only unpopular with the landowners, many in the Majlis, but was never implemented after Mosaddeq revealed its hidden agenda to swell the Pahlavi regime's coffers.

With the Shah's support, Alam began organizing a coup to overthrow Mosaddeq that was eventually to be given the code name Operation Ajax. Alam secretly met senior managers of both the AIOC and Standard Oil, knowing they would report back to Prime Minister Churchill and President Truman. To help Alam, the Shah gave him significant posts, such as the Chancellor of Shiraz University and Director of the Pahlavi Charitable Trust. It opened doors to influential people on the edge of government who were unsympathetic to Mosaddeq's policies. The coup would take much planning and would not come about until Eisenhower replaced Truman as President of the United States in January 1953.

Nine years after the success of Operation Ajax, the Shah finally made Alam prime minister in June 1962. He was appointed to root out corruption. With due diligence, his severe approach upset the landed gentry and the clerics. Prison sentences of up to five years, some in solitary confinement, were handed out without any appeal processes. Twelve army generals were investigated and either sacked or sent into exile. Members of the clergy were not exempt and accused of illegal financial activities. Alam's heavy-handed approach, with the Shah's full backing, further increased their unpopularity with the citizens at large. By 1963, riots were occurring in several cities led by Ayatollah Khomeini, a prominent Imam, involving tens of thousands of followers.

In Tehran, Alam called out the army to restore peace with the instructions "shoot to kill". Some 1,000 were either killed or injured, although the official figure was only eighty-six dead. Khomeini fled into exile, initially to Iraq, later to France. Alam retired in 1964 and died of cancer in 1978, one year before the Shah's overthrow that was to see Ayatollah Khomeini return and become Head of the Islamic State.

Princess Ashraf

The story that the old Shah had once called his son a weakling was, according to Soraya, untrue. Undeniably, Reza Khan Pahlavi expected total, unquestioning obedience from his children, all of whom were neglected by their parents.

Reza Khan had married four times. With three wives and twelve children to support, life was far from affluent, even on a general's salary. Things improved immeasurably when Reza Khan became Shah in 1926. Neither of his daughters' dysfunctional, arranged marriages lasted. Ashraf divorced Sahib Qavam in 1942.

By the end of WWII, Queen Fawzieh had divorced Mohammed Shah and left for Egypt. Therefore, Princess Shams should have become the first lady of Court, but she had divorced Djam and eloped to Cairo to marry her second husband, Ezatollah Minbashian.

Consequently, Ashraf, determined to take revenge for the slights she had suffered by being forced to marry Sahib Qavam, made herself indispensable to her brother. She became the centre of Iranian society and, together with her mother, the force behind the throne. Mosaddeq was to send her into exile for her vociferous opposition to his policy of nationalising the AIOC and Prime Minister Zahedi extended her so-called holiday for almost a year before allowing her return to Court. Two years later, after divorcing Qavam, she married Ahmad Shaiq with whom she had a son and a daughter. Divorced for the second time, she married Mehdi Bushehri in 1960 and died in Monte Carlo in 2016, aged ninety-six.

In 1947, she had gone to the Soviet Union as the head of a welfare charity. Received by Stalin, she stayed for three months studying their health and social systems. According to Krause, at this time, infant mortality in the poorest areas of Tehran was 80% and 20% of women were dying in childbirth. Illiteracy was 80%. The accuracy of many of Krause's statistics is questionable, however. In the same chapter, he says that Ashraf was married at fifteen and the marriage lasted six years; in fact, she was eighteen and it lasted only two years. On returning to Iran, she took the lead in fighting for women's rights, determined to stop husbands' time-marriages whenever it suited them. There are many quotes about Ashraf – "she should have been the Shah". Mosaddeq famously said, 'I thank Allah she is not the Shah.' Her reputation as the *enfant terrible* was such that he sent her into exile on more than one occasion.

Undoubtedly, both Ashraf and her sister were haunted by the ghost of their father who had demanded strict obedience. He had not only been an indifferent father to his daughters, but a despotic one too. Photos in the Pahlavi family album showed his son sitting on the Shah's knees, but with the two girls standing to one side looking unhappy. Ashraf and Shams struggled to tolerate each other as they grew up.

Ashraf's bitterness towards her sister strengthened her determination to succeed in whatever she undertook. Undoubtedly, she was the most gifted of Nimtaj al-Molouk's children. Coupled with unlimited energy and passion, Ashraf lived life at full-tilt. She didn't have time to listen to any vicious gossip about her; she despised everyone and did what she pleased.

10

LIVING WITH THE
PAHLAVIS

The Echtessassi Palace

Soon after returning from their Ramsar honeymoon to reside in the Echtessassi Palace, Soraya realised how badly it needed renovating. Since Queen Fawzieh's departure in 1945, the property and its household had been the responsibility of Princess Ashraf. However, she had her own home and had neglected her brother's house. Consequently, the Echtessassi's staff, most of who lived nearby, had progressively grown indifferent to the palace's rundown appearance with its ill-assorted furniture and no-one in charge.

The Shah encouraged Soraya to treat the palace as her own home. He gave her *carte blanche* to improve matters as she felt necessary, but with a limited budget.

Soraya's inspection of the accounts revealed money was disappearing that could not be traced. She found the kitchen in an unhygienic mess. Without hesitation, she fired the two cooks. That evening, she and the Shah dined at Shams' house. Soraya was astonished that her sister-in-law knew of the dismissal. One of Soraya's ladies-in-waiting, who had been recommended by Shams, was obviously a spy. Soraya's look of astonishment at the dinner table triggered an evasive explanation from her sister-in-law that she'd overheard the dismissal mentioned.

Later that evening, Soraya told the Shah and he agreed the maid should be dismissed. Shams never mentioned the incident again. The roots of suspicion about her in-laws' motives were growing ever stronger. She asked herself, "…surely the Shah must have known? Can I not trust my own husband?"

Soraya tackled the meals. She had found the food served to the Pahlavis consistently tasteless, unstimulating, and over-cooked. According to Fiona Ross in *Dining with the Rich and the Royals*, the Shah's father had apparently believed herbs and spices were the cause of his poor constitution. The Pahlavis were hypochondriacs, believing their austere diets were essential to remain healthy. The menus had, therefore, never been changed. Soraya discovered there were no condiments whatsoever in the Echtessassi, not even salt and pepper. She quickly gave the new chefs imaginative menus. Next, she paid attention to the Palace's milk supply. Tuberculosis had been found in the royal herd. At Soraya's insistence, new cows were imported from Switzerland. To Soraya's delight, she saw her husband putting on several pounds of weight. Furniture and curtains that had been in the palace since the Shah's boyhood were replaced. Walls were painted in bright, modern colours, with Soraya keeping within the Shah's budget.

Soraya's day would begin at nine o'clock. The Shah usually arose at 7.00am and went to his office in the Marble Palace. Consequently, she would breakfast alone. Afterwards, her Personal Private Secretary (PPS) would brief her on her diary: the protocols to be followed on her official duties and which lady-in-waiting would be in attendance. Invariably, it would entail a speech, drafted by her PPS. Soraya's Farsi improved rapidly as her PPS would help her with pronunciation and animation, although she retained her Lori accent to the end of her life.

Soraya's first meeting of the day with the Shah was generally at lunch. They always spoke to each other in the formal, third-person plural: equivalent to the French use of *vous* as opposed to the familiar, singular *tu*. From the very beginning of their marriage, even in private, they used the formal *vous*. When on the very rare occasions the Shah used the informal singular, Soraya knew something was amiss.

A regular duty was to entertain foreign attachés to afternoon tea. Most diplomats were impressed with her knowledge of their countries, but as the several hundred or so ambassadors were forever changing, it meant meeting almost one new diplomat each week. It gradually became a seemingly endless and somewhat tiresome task.

Two of Soraya's official positions were president of the tuberculosis isolation hospitals and the single-mother-and-child homes. Both organisations had lacked royal supervision since Queen Fawzieh's divorce. Soraya lost no time in gathering together all the doctors and managers who worked in both institutions. Discovering the scale of underfunding, she undertook regular inspections and called for weekly reports. She was determined to improve the lot of the patients – a task that she was to accomplish with aplomb. According to her cousin, her success is remembered to this day.

Loneliness

Dinner was always served at exactly 19.30 hours, whether together in the Echtessassi or elsewhere with the Shah's mother or his sisters. Occasionally, the entire Pahlavi family would be in attendance. Afterwards, they either watched a film or played endless card games. Soraya remarked in her biography that her marriage was already a mix of boredom and solitude. She added that while Shams wanted her friendship, Ashraf's coldness suggested she wanted her position.

Soraya was sickened that the Pahlavi women's gossip, when talking about members of the Court, was not only malicious but full of phrases riddled with unfathomable expressions. Having been brought up in a warm, sincere, loving family where there was no rivalry or struggle to impress, the Pahlavis' tittle-tattle upset her. Both her parents had taught her to treat others as she would wish them to treat her. The struggle for influence and status within the Pahlavi women was endemic. Soraya's loneliness left her feeling the only people she could trust in Court were Dr Ayadi and her aunt, Forough Zafar.

Less than two months after her wedding, the Shah, without warning, banned Forough Zafar from the Court. When Soraya objected, the Shah accused Forough of being a spy. Soraya laughed uncontrollably. The idea was ridiculous; she was picturing her jolly aunt – as wide as she was tall – but admitted in her biography that her aunt never minced her words. She challenged the Shah, 'Has Forough upset someone?' Met with an embarrassing silence, she persisted. However, her subsequent protests fell on death ears; he would not discuss the matter.

Soraya later discovered that it was the Shah's mother who had banned Forough from Court. Nimtaj believed Forough had launched Soraya's career by recommending Soraya. Therefore, Forough was at the centre of a Bakhtiari plot. Nimtaj had persuaded her son to believe her fantasy.

The loss of her trusted confident was a severe blow. She was now isolated. From the warmth of her family to the nastiness of the Pahlavis was akin to comparing heaven to hell. She began thinking that the Shah was having doubts about her suitability as his wife. The depressing thought made her wonder what her future as Empress might bring.

Holiday with the Shah

Every summer, the Pahlavis and the Court moved to Shemiran in the foothills of the Alborz Mountains to escape the heat of Tehran. They all resided at the Saadabad Palace complex, a 750-acre site built by the Qajar monarchs that included 400 acres of forest and a dozen detached residences. The Shah and Soraya always stayed at the White Palace, the largest and grandest villa. The couple went riding each day. They swam, played tennis and volleyball; Soraya watched her husband unwinding from the pressures of State.

Nimtaj Molouk

Soraya admitted in her autobiography that by the end of the summer of 1951, she realised the head of the whole Pahlavi dynasty was Nimtaj Molouk. She was a proud woman who had never forgotten that her father had created the reigning line. After all, it was her father who had commanded the Cossack regiment and promoted her husband to eventually become the Shah of Shahs.

Although Soraya, as Empress, was now senior in the hierarchy, it was Soraya and the Shah who always went to see Nimtaj, never the other way around. Nimtaj seemingly believed it was below her dignity to visit the Echtessassi. A decree promulgated by her husband, Reza Shah, without any consultation with the Majlis, had given only his two sons with Nimtaj the right to reign; the sons of his other wives could not inherit. She had acquired the same ruthless, arrogant personality as her ex-husband. Consequently, through her, the children still feared their father's presence. From her womb, all future Kings of Iran would be related.

Reza Khan had had four wives. Nimtaj accepted this as the norm, for she remained the senior wife. It was a situation that Soraya could neither understand nor come to accept.

Soraya sensed Nimtaj regretted her son had only one wife, as it made her position, as dowager, more difficult. Nimtaj's logic seemed to be that if her son had several wives, each with a number of children, then Soraya's position would be weakened as the sole empress. Although, theoretically, Nimtaj had no rights, in practice she knew of a thousand and one tricks to get her own way. She spent long hours drinking tea with her friends while discussing the latest gossip. She loved intrigue, and received foreign politicians as often as possible. She questioned them and listened to their chit-chat. She would then bend her son's ear if things needed changing. Soraya imagined the Shah saying, 'Yes, Mother, no, Mother.' Soraya wanted to believe her husband was not so easily taken in, but Nimtaj's influence in the Court never went away. Soraya, not going along with Nimtaj's games, was, therefore, cold-shouldered by her clique.

Soraya's official duties kept her busy, but she knew she was living in a spiteful matriarchy. After dinner with the family, Soraya had no option but to listen to Nimtaj's rantings. With Nimtaj's face quivering as she went into a tirade about some trivial Court matter, Soraya had to bite her tongue to prevent herself laughing. Nimtaj had become the mother-in-law from hell.

General Yazdan-Panah's wife, Leyla, the Royal Court's senior lady-in waiting, was privy to the blather. She often confided with her husband that the Shah's mother would frequently remark that it was Ashraf who had the balls in the family. Leyla told her husband that Nimtaj's resentment toward her daughter-in-law had grown to the point that it was common knowledge she didn't want Soraya as her son's only wife.

Soraya wrote in her second autobiography that the three women in the family "did not like to see me love the man I had to love". The words she chose, *had to love*, suggest her feelings for the Shah were already on the wane. She knew her sole *raison d'etre* was to procreate a Pahlavi heir.

Princess Shams

In 1945, Shams had eloped to Cairo with Ezatollah Minbashian, an architect who had studied at the University of Lausanne. He was the son of the conductor of the Tehran Symphony Orchestra. Seen as an unsuitable husband, the Shah exiled the couple after they married. Consequently, they moved to the United States for several years. In an attempt of reconciliation by the Shah, Shams and her husband were allowed to return to Iran in 1948 on condition that Minbashian changed his name and had no contact with his family. He took the name Merhdad Pahlbod.

Shams had returned to find her rightful place in society as the first lady of the Court hijacked by Ashraf who had shortly returned from three months in the Soviet Union. When Soraya appeared on the scene, she became something of a political football as Shams plotted and hatched schemes to be the favorite of the new Empress.

Ali Reza Pahlavi

Ali Reza Pahlavi was the Shah's younger brother. Born in 1922, and therefore two and a half years younger, he was first in line to the throne. He had attended the same Swiss school as his brother, but then settled in Paris with a beautiful Frenchwoman of Polish descent, Christiane Cholewski. There is no record of their marriage, but they had a son, Patrick Ali, who was born in September 1947. Later, Prince Ali Reza Pahlavi returned to Tehran alone. He was something of a recluse and lived with a girlfriend who Soraya never met. Nimtaj Molouk would not allow Ali's partner to attend Court. Not interested in the affairs of State, the couple moved back to Paris.

In theory, if he had he married Christiane, Patrick would have been second in line to the throne. After Prince Ali Reza was killed in a plane crash in October 1954, Patrick was arguably the first in line.

In 1970, Patrick moved from living in Paris to Iran, where he ruffled feathers by speaking publicly about the corruption of his uncle's regime. He was arrested and, theoretically, faced the death penalty. However, rather than being seen to pardon his nephew, the Shah quietly arranged his escape three days before his trial. Soraya's cousin thinks he went to Australia.

Other Minor Relatives

The Shah's eldest half-brother was Gholam, born to Reza Shah's third wife, Turan Amir. They had married in 1922. After Gholam was born, Reza Shah Pahlavi divorced her. In 1948, Gholam, aged twenty-five, married Homa Aalam. They had two children, a girl and a boy. However, after their daughter died, they split up. Homa remarried an engineer who constructed dams. A friend of Ashraf, Homa was allowed to return to Court and became friendly with Soraya.

The Shah had a half-sister, Fatima. She was born in 1928 to Reza Shah's fourth wife, Estmat Dowlatshahi, whom he had married in 1923. Against the Shah's orders, Fatima left Iran to marry an American, Lee Hillier, in 1948. Later, after Soraya's wedding, they divorced and Fatima married an Iranian pilot. Soraya had met her briefly when in Paris with Shams.

Fatima had three brothers – half-brothers to the Shah. The eldest was Abdul, who had studied politics at Harvard and married an American, Parissma Sand. The second brother, Ahmed, was a playboy according to Soraya. The third brother was Hamid, whose wife, Minou, was a relative of Mosaddeq. She divorced Hamid by having a clause inserted in their marriage contract to enact the divorce in front of an Imam.

Hamdam Pahlavi was born on 22nd February 1903 and was the eldest child of Reza Shah Pahlavi. Her mother, Maryam Savadkoohi, was Reza Khan's first wife but died when Hamdam was only one year old. Consequently, she was thirteen when her father married Nimtaj.

Hamdam married Hadi Atabay, and in 1925 bore her first child, Amir Reza Atabay. Later, she gave birth to two more children, Cyrus and Simin. Although a half-sister to the Shah, Soraya never met her. She died in 1992.

Princess Shahnaz

Princess Shahnaz was the daughter of the Shah and his first wife, Fawzieh. She was barely ten when the Shah and Soraya married. For five years, she had already been attending a boarding school in Switzerland – hardly ever seeing her father and never her mother. She came to spend her first summer with Soraya at Saadabad where her body language made it obvious she saw Soraya as an intruder for her father's affection.

However, the ice between them melted slowly as they walked, played tennis with the Shah, and went swimming. At the end of her summer holiday, Shahnaz allowed Soraya to accompany her back to school. Soraya spotted Shahnaz admiring a ring she was wearing and offered it to her. It was an inspired gesture, for as Shahnaz entered the school, proudly wearing the ring, she shyly asked Soraya when she would return to see her. Thereafter, they remained firm friends.

11

THE INNOCENT EMPRESS

The Rude Awakening

Soraya's experience as empress was not what she had expected. Her imagined lifestyle, based on the love of romantic films, did not exist. There were no grand moonlight balls with unlimited champagne. There was little laughter or happiness in the Pahlavi Court.

Doubts about the wisdom of her becoming empress were compounded whenever she awoke in the morning to find the space next to her in bed was cold. Her husband would go to work without saying goodbye. Frequently, he slept in his private quarters with its lounge, bathroom and office. On such occasions, she wouldn't see the Shah until the following evening. She never asked why; she reluctantly accepted it as part of her job.

Many of her days were spent visiting hospitals, orphanages, and people's homes. There, she met poverty and squalor on an unimaginable scale. The houses typically had no running water; where it did, it was often dirty. Toilets were frequently communal. Children, 80% of them illiterate, commonly had rickets. Tuberculosis was rampant, particularly among the elderly.

The Shah would listen to Soraya's stories over dinner. His sympathy appeared to be genuine and his face would go pale, but his explanation was always that the State's coffers were empty. He would fall silent and Soraya would hold his hand, not knowing what to believe as she watched his crocodile tears. If his workload permitted, they would drive around Tehran with Soraya pointing out where she had seen the hopelessness of its citizens. The Shah would shake his head in apparent disbelief but would say nothing nor do anything.

Tainted Holiday

Since unwillingly appointing Mosaddeq as Prime Minister in April 1951, the Shah's depression had steadily worsened. Ministers, who had previously consulted him on affairs of State, were now referring to Mosaddeq for decisions. Her husband was feeling unwanted and Soraya was at her wits' end. She asked Dr Ayadi for help. She learned that her husband had suffered with duodenum problems before they met. Peron, Ashraf and Nimtaj had insisted the Shah's intestinal problems had been kept secret from the Court. Furthermore, the Shah had refused to have an operation, believing his problems were psychosomatic. However, by August 1951, just six months after their wedding, the Shah fell seriously ill with suspected peritonitis.

Dr Ayadi consulted American specialists who diagnosed the cause of the Shah's pain as an abnormal hardening of his duodenum. Immediate surgery was essential, and American surgeons arrived to carry out the operation. Afterwards, they told Soraya that it was 'a particularly strange case'. They told her that unexplained cysts had been removed, but didn't amplify. While he recovered, Soraya remained at his bedside day and night. Her health suffered with worry and she lost weight. Having to tolerate her scheming in-laws didn't help. Soraya was missing the warmth of her parents and came close to a nervous breakdown.

As the weeks passed, the Shah began to get stronger and could see Soraya badly needed a break. He insisted she should visit her mother in Switzerland. Under protest, she flew to Zurich with a lady-in-waiting and Princess Shanaz, who was returning to boarding school. Within a week, her mother's menus, walks in the mountains, and learning to laugh again helped her recovery. She temporary forgot Tehran and its troubles.

Each evening, the Shah telephoned her and insisted she prolonged her break to fully regain her strength – a strange request that she would discover many years later may have had an ulterior motive.

Soraya and her mother decided to take a holiday in Spain for two weeks. With the sun shining every day, walks in the flower markets, meandering in the bric-a-brac shops, and smelling fish as it was cooked for them in the alfresco bistros fully restored her health.

Away for almost a month, she returned to Tehran to find petrol stations no longer had signs in English; they were solely in Farsi. The streets were full of optimism – everyone believed oil would soon be free.

Living back in the Echtessassi, Soraya had expected Dr Ayadi to visit her and check on her recovery. She was puzzled when he never came. After two days, she asked the Shah for an explanation. The Shah, embarrassed, apologised and said Ayadi had been dismissed. Having previously lost Forough Zafar, Dr Ayadi had been her one true friend left in Court. Seeing his wife's distress, the Shah explained Ayadi was from a Baha'i family – a sect that believed in the unity of all monotheistic religions. The Imams were preaching this was heresy that was endangering the country. Riots had created a state of turmoil with hundreds killed. The Shah had been persuaded that removing Dr Ayadi was for his own safety.

For Soraya, it was a massive blow. Soraya strongly suspected that Peron and Nimtaj were at the bottom of the plot to remove Dr Ayadi. She was barely nineteen years old and was now totally alone in the Court.

Early Troubles with Mosaddeq

Mosaddeq had always been courteous to Soraya. He had whispered to her in Lori, when they first met, that they were both Bakhtiaris. While giving her a smile and a sly wink, he'd told her that, therefore, they were distantly related, and their heritage was much superior to the rest of the Court. A great orator, his speeches to the Majlis held everyone's attention. He would weep when evoking memories of Persia's great past, and laugh when poking fun at the Qajar dynasty's appalling record of misrule. A brilliant intellectual, he was a fanatical nationalist, able to carry the masses with him.

After nationalising the AIOC on 1ˢᵗ May 1951, the British took him to the International Court of Justice at The Hague. On 9ᵗʰ June, he pleaded his case in impeccable French at The Hague. The AIOC was accused of not allowing the Iranians to examine the quantities of oil being extorted from their fields nor of discovering the price the AIOC received from its sales. Their possession of all the technical installations and pipelines, he claimed, was a matter for Iranian jurisdiction.

Listening to his speech on Tehran Radio, Soraya knew that the British Royal Navy was patrolling the Persian Gulf sequestrating all ships carrying Iranian oil. As a consequence, the economy was collapsing. Iranian engineers were incapable of maintaining Abadan. Spares were unavailable, the pipelines were clogging up, the docks were empty and poverty was returning to pre-WWII levels.

The mood of the people resulted in protests blaming the Shah for their troubles. Afraid of riots, he slept with a revolver under his pillow. He would change their bedroom each evening to increase security. Although the Shah had welcomed nationalising the oil industry, he was a pragmatist and had been more aware of the difficulties of selling the oil than anyone else. Soraya didn't realise that the conflict between her husband and Mosaddeq would escalate to the extent of not only ruining both their lives, but Iran as well.

Whenever Soraya met Mosaddeq, he often repeated that he would never forget what Mohammed Shah Pahlavi had done for him when releasing the political prisoners in 1941. Soraya admitted, the Shah secretly had a high regard for him. She thought the Shah and Mosaddeq both wanted greatness for Iran, but a seismic collision between the two was inevitable.

12

THE MOSADDEQ AFFAIR

Time Magazine's **Man of the Year**

The repercussions of the Mosaddeq Affair and Soraya's divorce were unquestionably the two most important events that led to the Shah's downfall. Mosaddeq was the most gifted and talented Iranian Minister of all time, while Soraya's popularity with the masses knew no bounds. The Shah's eventual enforced exile from Iran created the Islamic State that affects current Iranians' day-to-day lives.

In 1951, US President Harry Truman, General Dwight Eisenhower, Prime Minister Winston Churchill and Mohammed Mosaddeq were shortlisted to become *Time Magazine's* "Man of the Year". The magazine's choice to select Mosaddeq surprised many in the western world. It was the result of the two major western powers' version of history that hid and buried the achievements of Iran's Prime Minister. *Time Magazine* called him Iran's "George Washington. Like George Washington, he threw the British out of his country".

Timeline of Events

7th **March 1951** – The assassination of Prime Minister Razmara and the growing movement to nationalise the AIOC brought chaos in Iran. Mosaddeq, after his re-election to the Majlis, began consolidating his position, using the freedom of the press to cast doubts about the Shah's loyalty to the people.

20th **March 1951** – In the Majlis, Mosaddeq's resolution to nationalise the oil industry was passed unanimously. Prime Minister Hussein Ala had to resign as Prime Minister. The next day, the Majlis voted Mosaddeq Prime Minister by seventy-nine votes to six.

28th **April 1951** – With Mosaddeq's popularity riding high in both the Majlis and the country, the Shah was left with no choice. He had to formally appoint Mosaddeq as Prime Minister. Nonetheless, the Shah remained firmly of the belief that a compromise solution with the AIOC was preferable to outright nationalisation. Despite Princess Ashraf and Nimtaj reminding the Shah of the problems his father had had in 1925 when Mosaddeq opposed the dissolution of the Qajar dynasty, the Shah knew there was no alternative but to give Mosaddeq a free rein.

1st **May 1951** – Mosaddeq announced his intention to nationalise the AIOC by cancelling the existing 1933 agreement that wasn't due to finish until 1993. The AIOC would be compensated for the expropriation of its assets by receiving 25% of the net oil profits. A week later, the AIOC took Iran to the International Court of Justice at The Hague. Mosaddeq's other proposals included his intention to introduce unemployment benefit, sick pay for injuries at work, and freeing peasants from forced labour on their landlords' estates. He drafted a Land Reform Act that would force landlords to give 20%

of their profits to pay for local projects such as public baths, libraries and housing. The *New York Times* praised his personal integrity, for he turned down his official limousine and salary as Prime Minister to distribute it to the poor.

9th June 1951 – Mosaddeq pleaded his country's case at The Hague. "The oil resources of Iran are like its soil, rivers and mountains – they are the property of the people of Iran." He alternated statements with jokes that ridiculed the British for trying to persuade the world that the lamb had devoured the wolf.

Mosaddeq claimed that the AIOC was a "State within a State"; everything was in the hands of the British Government.

22nd July 1951 – The International Court of Justice ruled by a vote of 9 to 5 that it had no jurisdiction in the British-Iranian dispute over oil nationalisation. The verdict ended Britain's hopes of getting a judgment against Iran. A British spokesman declared Britain would persist in stopping tankers carrying oil produced at the AIOC's sites. The President of the International Court was British. Sir Arnold Duncan McNair voted for the majority decision and it was the first time in the history of the court that a judge had voted against his own government.

30th July 1951 – The AIOC offered to increase the percentage of oil profits to 55%. Mosaddeq, now in a stronger position than ever, refused. The Shah tried to get Mosaddeq to accept, but failed. The AIOC withdrew their employees. The Shah confided with Soraya that as the people thought he had approved Mosaddeq's policy, he had lost his status and they should think of going abroad.

September 1951 – The Shah had an operation for peritonitis, triggered by depression. Soraya grew so depressed that with the

Shah recovering, he encouraged Soraya to have a holiday and visit her mother in Switzerland. A month later, Soraya returned from her holiday to find Mosaddeq had gone to the UN in New York to plead that the Royal Navy's blockade was illegal. The UN Security Council's vote was indecisive. On 17ᵗʰ October, the representative of Ecuador submitted a draft resolution: *"The Security Council, deciding on the question of its own competence, advises the parties concerned to reopen negotiations as soon as possible with a view to making a fresh attempt to settle their differences in accordance with the Purposes and Principles of the United Nations Charter."* Mosaddeq met US President Truman and asked for a loan. He received $23.5 million, a quarter of what he wanted.

November 1951 – The Shah met Mosaddeq to plead accepting the 55% offer. Mosaddeq refused "to agree to sell our birthright for mere potage". However, the Iranian oil industry was grinding to a halt. Making the situation worse was the newly formed British Petroleum and American oil companies doubling their production in Saudi Arabia. Mosaddeq told the Shah he was going to introduce an electoral reform bill that would give one man one vote regardless of their class or education. It was a revolutionary idea, as illiterate men could not vote.

January 1952 – Mosaddeq organised anti-British demonstrations in Tehran and the British Embassy closed. Mosaddeq accused all the Pahlavis of being in league with the British and Americans. Averell Harriman, US Secretary of Commerce, visited Tehran and offered international aid to get reconstruction of the oil industry restarted. Mosaddeq refused.

May 1952 – Soraya persuaded the Shah to take a break at Saadabad. Soraya hoped the atmosphere would relax her husband. The

American ambassador, Loy Henderson, visited the Shah suggesting further compromises to settle the West's differences with Mosaddeq's government. When the Shah put the new proposals to Mosaddeq, he was greeted with, "Your job is to reign, not to rule."

July 1952 – Mosaddeq declared a state of emergency and demanded total control of the Majlis for six months. The Shah refused to surrender his position as Commander-in-Chief of the armed forces. Mosaddeq resigned. The Shah appointed a new Prime Minister, Ahmed Ghavam, who declared his opposition to nationalising the oil industry. Strikes broke out in all of the major towns. Fearful of the troops' support for Mosaddeq, the Shah ordered the army to withdraw to their barracks. The riots worsened. Four days later, and having lost total support in the Majlis, Ghavam resigned and Mosaddeq returned, stronger than ever. The Shah had to bow down to Mosaddeq's demands and granted him control of the army. Mosaddeq had become Iran's uncontested leader. Not all army officers agreed and those known to favour the Shah's leadership were dismissed, including the most popular – General Zahedi.

Although Mosaddeq was not a member of the communist party, trade with the USSR increased three-fold, while declining with the West. Mosaddeq reduced the Shah's allowance and stopped his contact with foreign diplomats. The same week in Cairo, King Farouk was overthrown by General Naguib and Colonel Nasser. It left the Shah wondering if he was next. He discussed leaving Iran with Soraya, but when she asked where, when, and for how long, he had no reply.

3rd August 1952 – Mosaddeq exiled the Shah's mother and Princess Ashraf on the grounds that they were plotting treason. Princess Shams, who had not been ordered into exile, took her mother to California along with her husband and children. Princess Ashraf flew to Paris.

November 1952 – MI6, on Churchill's instructions, began exchanging signals with the Central Intelligence Agency (CIA) that Mosaddeq must be ousted and further began planning Operation Ajax, the coup to remove Mosaddeq.

20th January 1953 – President Eisenhower became 34th President of the United States and American policy towards Iran changed. Eisenhower agreed to support Britain's line, refusing any further aid to Iran until the dispute was resolved. Mosaddeq, sensing the shift in American policy, extended his emergency powers for a further year. He set up a system of collective farming with land owned by the government that weakened the landed aristocracy. However, the Iranians were becoming poorer by the day and Mosaddeq's political coalition was beginning to crumble.

The Shah decided to abdicate and leave Iran. Mosaddeq agreed, offering to pay all travel expenses providing the Shah's entourage travelled overland to Beirut so everyone thought he was leaving for a winter sports holiday. Soraya had no regrets about exile – she had been through so much in her two years of marriage, but kept her thoughts to herself. Life as a deposed Empress would be less taxing, she thought, whether in America or the South of France.

28th February 1953 – On the eve before leaving, Soraya received an envoy from Ayatollah Kashani, the Head of Iran's religious leaders. The messenger handed her a letter explaining that Kashani, previously a supporter of Mosaddeq, wanted Soraya to exercise all her influence with the Shah to stay. Kashani was worried that with the Shah gone, Mosaddeq would let the communists come to power and Islam would be replaced by atheism. Unknown to Soraya, the letter had been widely distributed among the anti-Mosaddeq underground.

1st March 1953 – Early in the morning, Mosaddeq arrived at the

Echtessassi to say farewell to the Shah and Soraya. He was in a hurry to see them off, having been briefed there may be demonstrations later that day by Kashani supporters. However, as the Shah and Mosaddeq were exchanging civilities, noisy shouts were being heard outside. Kashani's supporters were already on the streets surrounding the Echtessassi Palace and calling for the Shah to stay. Soraya described Mosaddeq going deathly pale. Feeling sorry for him, she took his hand and whispered that if he went out through the back door, he would escape the crowds. Mosaddeq sensibly beat a retreat. Boosted by Kashani's unexpected support, the Shah addressed the crowd from an Echtessassi balcony and promised to remain in Tehran.

Nonetheless, Mosaddeq remained head of the government, and soon his supporters were back on the streets. Fighting and its consequent bloodshed broke out. In attempting to quell the riots, the chief of police was captured, his body mutilated and dumped on waste ground.

Unknown to the Shah, US Secretary of State, John Foster Dulles, approved the CIA plan to remove Mosaddeq. Operation Ajax was underway.

4th **April 1953** – The CIA were given $1,000,000 by Eisenhower to finance the coup, beginning with radio propaganda criticising Mosaddeq's handling of Iran's problems and accusing him of being a Jew and a communist.

Soraya Leaves Iran

17th **April 1953** – The riots in Tehran had become so bad that the Shah insisted Soraya went to Europe, promising he would recall her as soon as the crisis was over. Soraya flew to Rome with her maid and Personal Private Secretary. They were met by her mother. The paparazzi followed them everywhere and severely curtailed their social life. Some weeks later, they went to Madrid. Invited to lunch with Franco, Soraya met his daughter, Carmen, and they became lifelong friends. The press continued to follow Soraya everywhere. Noting her unhappiness, they dubbed her the Empress with sad eyes. The rumour of a divorce spread like wildfire. Again attempting to flee the paparazzi, Soraya and Eva went to Cannes at the beginning of June, but to no effect. After a fortnight, Soraya gave up trying to avoid the press; she realised she would receive less attention in Tehran. Despite the Shah wishing her to remain in the South of France, Soraya, with her two members of staff, returned on 15th June.

13

FLEEING IRAN

Soraya's Decisiveness

Contrary to the story she had been getting told by the Shah, Soraya, on her return, found the political situation relatively quiet – definitely safer than when she had left two months previously. It didn't occur to her to ask her husband why he had not wanted her to come home.

Ayatollah Kashani and several influential members of the Majlis had formed an effective opposition to Mosaddeq's National Party. However, Soraya discovered her husband had been doing very little in her absence; simply hoping the opposition would grow strong enough to overthrow Mosaddeq. Her twenty-first birthday went unnoticed. On the other hand, Mosaddeq, aware of the potential threat, made an intuitive decision to bring forward his snap referendum. The Shah wrote to Mosaddeq pointing out that it was against the constitution, as only he could call an election. Mosaddeq replied that the ultimate decision must rest with the people and announced it would be held on 12th August.

25th June 1953 – Soraya was seeing the consequences of cutting off all US aid to Iran. She knew oil production had fallen to an all-time low;

the largest oil refinery in the world at Abadan had closed. Poverty was getting worse by the day. She demanded her husband grab the bull by the horns.

She pleaded that the longer they waited, the worse the situation would get. She suggested that to save the country, he must organise a revolt directed against Mosaddeq.

The Shah refuted the idea, retorting that no monarch had ever plotted against his own country. She was angry with him. Realising he was procrastinating yet again, she told him he must remove Mosaddeq's government, for no one else would. Soraya's outburst was probably heresy. She admitted in her biography that she lost her temper with him. She demanded he stopped moping and become the man she had once admired. She suggested that if he didn't act, Mosaddeq would end up selling his country to Moscow.

Shocked by his wife's ferocity, the Shah consulted his closest and most trusted advisers. All advised him to wait and see. However, when he learnt that Mosaddeq had secured the support of the Soviet Ambassador for his referendum and that the Tudeh would assist in its organisation, there was no choice. He realised Soraya was right and that only one man could oust Mosaddeq – General Zahedi.

Zahedi, when twenty-eight, had been the youngest general in the Army and was something of a legendary figure. A favourite of Reza Shah, he had been in charge of crushing internal revolts, such as that of the Bakhtiaris before WWII.

1st **July 1953** – Soraya and the Shah met Colonel Nassiri, Commander of the Imperial Lifeguards, at their palace in Ramsar. The three drew up a plan of action to win Zahedi's support – not easy, as he was permanently in hiding. Mosaddeq had put a bounty on his head of 100,000 rials. Luckily, Nassiri was friendly with Zahedi's son, Ardeshir, and agreed to approach him. Ardeshir agreed to send a message to his father. The general immediately supported the plan for the Shah to write a decree dismissing Mosaddeq and appoint Zahedi as Prime Minister. Zahedi's emissary would deliver the letter after the referendum result's had been announced, by which time Zahedi's troops would have seized all the key points of Tehran, so taking Mosaddeq's men by surprise.

CIA Involvement

3rd July 1953 – Meanwhile, the CIA's plot to overthrow Mosaddeq was taking shape. They organized a classic false-flag operation. They paid Iranian operatives to pretend being pro-Mosaddeq thugs. By threatening the pro-Shah Imams with violence if they didn't support Mosaddeq, the Imams became ever more vehement in their support of the Shah. The idea to stir anti-Mosaddeq sentiments within the religious community worked perfectly. Other CIA lackeys were spreading the rumour in the bazaars that Mosaddeq was a Jew planning to set up a communist state. The CIA paid Princess Ashraf to return from France, hoping that she would stiffen her brother's resolve to carry through the coup. When Mosaddeq heard, his police arrested her as she arrived at the airport and sent her straight back to France.

11th July 1953 – Mosaddeq called his ministers together and informed them when he intended to dissolve parliament before the August elections.

13th – 15th July 1953 – Riots broke out unchecked. The demonstrators neither knew who they were fighting for, nor why they were on the streets. No one was in control. Mosaddeq supporters thought the chaos would end the Pahlavi dynasty, as they and the Tudeh party were better organised than the Imams' supporters.

20th July 1953 – General Herbert Schwarzkopf (his son Norman led the coalition forces during Operation Desert Storm that ousted Saddam Hussein's forces from Kuwait in 1991) appeared unannounced in Tehran. Previously, in 1941, the young Shah had chosen Schwarzkopf to modernise Iran's security services. Schwarzkopf had appointed Zahedi as his assistant. Without asking the Shah, Zahedi had sought Schwarzkopf's help as he needed him to become the essential link with the CIA. The joint operation is generally thought to have been led by the CIA, but in both of Soraya's biographies she stresses that it was she who persuaded the Shah, which sparked off the overthrow of Mosaddeq.

22ⁿᵈ July – 10ᵗʰ August 1953 – The chaos in Tehran increased as pro- and anti-monarchists, both paid by the CIA, clashed. Mosques were looted and burnt. The death toll increased to over 300.

Soraya relates that the Shah remained indecisive and admitted to her he had doubts as to whether he should dismiss Mosaddeq. She claimed that at one point she yelled at him that he was "a pitiful coward".

11ᵗʰ August 1953 – The Shah finally signed the *firman* – the decree to sack Mosaddeq – and handed it to Nassiri for delivery after the forthcoming referendum results. Soraya and her husband flew from Tehran to Chalus, on the Caspian Sea. Ostensibly, it was for a short holiday. In reality, it was for their safety at Zahedi's insistence, while he planned the organisation of his troops. The couple's only communication with Tehran was a secret radio transmitter connected to Colonel Nassiri's headquarters. The telephone lines were not secure.

12ᵗʰ August 1953 – The referendum asked the people did they agree to Mosaddeq's dissolution of parliament. The "Yes" voters went to Cannon Square, the "No" voters to Bahristan Square. Only 1,300 voted "No"; 2,043,300 supposedly voted "Yes". The rigged result gave the CIA an excuse to remove Mosaddeq.

13ᵗʰ August 1953 – Colonel Nassiri handed over the Shah's dismissal order to Mosaddeq but was arrested. Zahedi's plan had been betrayed by an unknown double agent. However, Zahedi had been warned and gone underground.

15ᵗʰ August 1953 – Nassiri's Imperial Guard tried to arrest all the members of Mosaddeq's cabinet. It failed miserably and Mosaddeq quickly regained control. Mass demonstrations in the capital wanted the Shah to be arrested. When Soraya and her husband received the bad news, the Shah sank into a deep depression as he remembered the similar overthrow of his former brother-in-law, King Farouk of Egypt. Soraya tried to cheer him up, assuring him that while Zahedi was safe, there was hope.

16ᵗʰ August 1953 – The Shah knew it was time to go. At 4.00am on Sunday morning, the Shah entered Soraya's bedroom and told her that Mosaddeq had won and they must leave at once. Soraya packed a few essentials and hurriedly climbed aboard their Bonanza aircraft. He explained they were flying to Ramsar where the Shah had a twin-engine Beechcraft. Their Bonanza's range was insufficient to reach Iraq's capital, over 750 miles away. The Beechcraft would take them to Baghdad.

Mosaddeq went on Radio Tehran and announced that a coup directed against the democratically elected government had been thwarted and arrests were being made. Mosaddeq said the Shah had abdicated. The traitor Zahedi, Mosaddeq proclaimed, had escaped, but there was a 500,000 rials (about $150,000) reward for information leading to his arrest.

14

ESCAPE TO ROME

Baghdad, Sunday, 16th August 1953

At 6.00am, the twin-engine Vickers Beechcraft departed Ramsar with the Shah's personal pilot and two aides-de-camp. All four men were deeply depressed. The Shah was repeatedly mumbling that it was all over. Ever positive and trying to buck-up his spirits, Soraya tried to assure him that they would be back in Tehran within a month.

The Shah could only shake his head.

Soraya reminded him that Zahedi was free and had the backing of the CIA. She told him the Americans will see the end of Mosaddeq. He must remain positive for the sake of his country.

Towards noon, they saw the mosques of Baghdad, and the Shah's pilot asked for permission to land.

The air traffic control tower demanded identification.

The pilot gave the identification of the aircraft and made out that they had lost an engine. He made no mention of the passengers aboard.

The unscheduled flight was allowed to land but directed to a far corner of the airfield, well away from the arrival and departure buildings. No sooner had the Beechcraft's engines come to a stop than a jeep arrived full of armed police to surround the aeroplane. The Shah and Soraya were to learn that the King of Iraq had been expected to arrive at any minute from an official visit in the north of his country. The sudden appearance of an unknown aircraft had caused considerable alarm in the air traffic control tower.

They waited in the Beechcraft for a while until the Shah took the initiative, left the aircraft and greeted the senior police officer in Arabic. He handed him a written note to be passed to King Faisal II as soon as possible. The police officer grunted and, not recognising him, took the note without looking at it. Without replying, he ushered the Iranian party into a nearby wooden hut.

The Shah and Soraya saw King Faisal's plane land and watched him review a guard of honour on the far-side of the airfield. Half an hour passed in the stifling heat, over 40°C, before the airport manager arrived. He immediately recognised the Shah, apologised and explained the hold-up. He escorted the party to an air-conditioned waiting room in the main airport building and offered them coffee while ringing the King's Palace. The contrast between the oven conditions in the airfield hut and the blast of the air conditioning was sufficient for Soraya to catch a chill.

A further hour past before the Minister for Foreign Affairs, Khalil Kenna, appeared and took them to a government guest house to freshen up. By five o'clock, they were driven, accompanied by Kenna, to the royal palace to have tea with King Faisal. Concerned that her crumpled linen dress was unsuitable to present herself to the king, she asked Kenna before leaving whether she was sufficiently presentable.

He reputedly replied that his majesty was aware she had not come from a fashion show. Wounded by his tactless riposte, she felt that the Iraqi minister saw her as a model rather than an empress.

Faisal greeted them with kindness and offered asylum indefinitely. He pointed out that the Iranian ambassador to Baghdad had already heard of their arrival. Having informed Mosaddeq, there was already a

Courtesy Alamy
Soraya arriving in Baghdad feeling dishevelled.

diplomatic demand for their return. After discussing the implications of remaining in Iraq, they thanked the king for his offer but decided they must move on. They stayed in Baghdad that night organised a private plane, and flew to Rome, accompanied with the Shah's two aides, the next day.

Rome, Monday, 17th August 1953

On arrival at Rome Airport, they were met by several members of the Italian Government, along with dozens of press photographers. Notable by his absence was the Iranian Ambassador to Italy, Nezam Nouri, who had nailed his colours to Mosaddeq's mast. In Rome, they were accommodated in the Excelsior Hotel where an Iranian industrialist had vacated a fourth-floor suite of rooms for the couple. Later, when restored to his throne, the Shah suitably rewarded the businessman for his kindness. They spent most of the day recovering from fatigue. However, with an estimated 200 paparazzi swarming in the front of the hotel, they managed to escape by a rear door to buy some personal effects, including Soraya's famous red polka-dot dress. It is still believed to be the most photographed dress of all time with 200 paparazzi each taking between thirty and forty photos of Soraya in her vivid, eye-catching frock.

Rumour was widespread that the Shah had abdicated and would join his former brother-in-law, Farouk, in Capri. That evening, the couple listened to Tehran Radio as the Iranian Foreign Minister Fatemi made a speech denouncing the Shah as capricious, bloodthirsty, and a servant of the British. Fatemi, the editor of one of Tehran's daily newspapers, proposed all Pahlavis should be hanged and a republic declared.

Tehran Radio described hundreds of buildings being looted, including the mausoleum of the Shah's father. All over Tehran, mobs were tearing down pictures of the Shah and burning them. Soraya admitted that even she, normally so optimistic, gave up hope. The pair discussed their future and the Shah expressed his preference to live in America, hoping all of his family – mother, brothers and sisters – would be spared and they could all live together.

Parsimonious Future

It was generally believed the Pahlavis were extremely wealthy. According to Soraya's biographies, the problem was that their wealth lay in land originally acquired by Reza Shah. The estates produced an income that would be confiscated if Iran became a republic. Unlike the monach in the United Kingdom, whose whole family are on a civil list, in Iran the Shah was the only royal to receive a State salary. Soraya estimated it was about $250,000 per annum, from which he had to meet the expenses of the Court as well as provide for his family. Their future, Soraya admitted, looked bleak. The assertion of paucity is hard to believe when the lavish lifestyle of the Pahlavis and their Court is examined.

Having discussed the wealth of the Shah with Soraya's cousin, I was assured the Shah eventually became a billionaire when he began receiving 5% of the total sale of Iranian oil. The money, she told me, was laundered through his relatives and trusted friends who were in sensitive jobs and positions. Forty-three years after the Shah's death, his relatives, including his third wife, still live in exceptional luxury. Today, her private secretary has to daily invest the interest that has accrued on Queen Farah's wealth from the previous day. The cousin assured me that the daily sums involved are several million US dollars. The cousin's ex-husband was at one time a high ranking diplomat in the

Getty Images
The famous red polka dot dress

Washington embassy. She assured me the lavish entertainment given at their embassy was legendary. Each month, countless kilograms of caviar arrived to be presented on a silver platter, decorated with a life-sized ice-statue of a swan for guests to help themselves. Champagne was unlimited. In Soraya's biographies, Soraya states her husband did not have a numbered Swiss bank account, for, if he had, she would have known. For whatever reason, the Shah was pulling the wool over her eyes.

At a late lunch in the hotel, two o'clock in Rome – half-past four in Tehran – a young reporter from Associated Press (AP) approached them. He handed the Shah a copy of a dispatch that had just arrived on the agency's teleprinter. It read,

MOSADDEQ OVERTHROWN – IMPERIAL TROOPS CONTROL TEHRAN – GENERAL ZAHEDI PRIME MIISTER

Unable to believe the news, they continued to finish their lunch while the AP reporter flitted back and forth to his office bringing updates. Radio Tehran had stopped transmission, so the Shah asked the hotel manager to tune into Radio Cairo that was relaying messages from Tehran. They learnt that Fatemi had been assassinated and his body hacked to pieces in the street. The offices of his newspaper had been ransacked and burnt down. Mosaddeq had been arrested.

Apparently, Schwarzkopf had spent $10,000,000 of CIA funds to raise a reserve of men, gathered from the unemployed, to ravage Mosaddeq's supporters and control the city.

A second cousin of Khalil, Teymour Bakhtiar, was a brigadier in charge of Iran's Second Armoured Brigade in Kermanshah, a town approximately 250 miles west of Tehran. He had moved his brigade east on his own initiative to support Zahedi. His advance towards Tehran at the head of an armoured column was one of the decisive factors in helping to crush Mosaddeq's Party and the communist elements in the country. Thereafter, the result had never been in doubt. The people had begun to believe Mosaddeq was prepared to use the communists for usurping power. The idea of their country becoming an atheist republic on Soviet lines was an anathema to them. There is no evidence that Mosaddeq was directly involved in the mob vandalizing the old Shah's mausoleum, seen as sacred, but the people blamed him. Red flags, prominent when the Shah and Soraya had fled, were now in flames. Ayatollah Kashani had whipped up support from the faithful who were appearing on the streets. The simultaneous arrival of the Zahedi's supporters, the CIA's lackeys and Teymour Bakhtiari's troops from Kermanshah sealed Mosaddeq's fate.

Shouts of "Long live Zahedi" and "God save the Shah" filled the streets. When Zahedi drove a tank to the front of the police headquarters where a battle was raging between the police and demonstrators, the fighting stopped. The police surrendered. Mosaddeq was alone. He surrendered to Zahedi the following morning.

On Wednesday, 19th August, the Excelsior Hotel switchboard was jammed by telephone calls from across the world. As the flood of telegrams and messages increased, Soraya saw her husband becoming a different man with his confidence growing exponentially.

At dinner on the hotel terrace, the Shah told Soraya she was to remain in Rome while he returned to Iran. He used the informal *tu* and said it firmly. There was to be no discussion. Upset, Soraya felt she had shared the bad times with him and given him her full support, without which he may have been overwhelmed. Her reaction was to think she could be getting cast aside.

Seeing he had upset her, he held her hand and looked into her eyes. He returned to the formal *vous* to explain it was for her safety. He may have been temporarily forgiven, but the episode was never forgotten.

Rome, Thursday, 20th August 1953

Zahedi's telegram had arrived shortly before dawn, owing to the time difference between Tehran and Rome. The Shah had been called out of bed to receive it. In reply, he sent a proclamation to the Iranian people and a telegram to General Zahedi.

General Zahedi's telegram to the Shah read: *The Iranian people, and your devoted Army, are awaiting your return with the greatest impatience and are counting the minutes. I beg you to hasten your journey back in order that your people may show you their sentiments as they so ardently wish to do.*

The Shah's proclamation declared, *In the name of the Almighty, I am profoundly grateful for the support that the Iranian people have shown toward me. In defence of the constitution, I hereby call on all members of the armed forces, all civilian officials and all the people to obey the orders of the Premier, His Excellency General Zahedi. He is constitutionally designated by me to lead the legitimate National Government of Iran. Long Live Iran and the Iranian people.*

The Shah's personal reply to General Zahedi read: *Your telegram was received with the utmost pleasure. It is impossible for me to tell you how anxious I am to return to my beloved country. With a heart full of joy for a bright future, I will leave Rome for Baghdad as soon as possible. From there, I will proceed to my country, whose people and Army have always proved to be so devoted and courageous.*

The Shah and Queen Soraya were joined by Princess Ashraf. She had flown from Switzerland, officially to act as a companion for Soraya, who had been feeling unwell. A physician diagnosed a severe headache and exhaustion. However, she improved considerably during the day and was able to dine that evening with the Shah and his sister, who was publicly indulging in the euphoria at the hotel.

Being unable to return with the Shah was a kick in the teeth. After all, without her support, the Shah would have lost his throne.

Before leaving Rome that evening, already Friday in Tehran, the Shah sacked Nouri as his ambassador to Italy. The Shah boarded a Royal Dutch KLM Constellation, charted from Amsterdam. He was on his way to Baghdad, where he was to transfer to the private plane that he had used to flee Iran. Wanting maximum publicity for himself as the conquering hero, the Shah insisted on having twenty reporters and photographers accompany him. He threatened to end the airline's concession to fly over Iran unless the newsmen were authorized to board the plane for its 1,659-mile flight to Baghdad.

Rome, Friday, 21st August 1953

On Friday, Eva arrived to be with her daughter. A day later, Soraya's maid arrived from Tehran with one of Soraya's dogs. Sightseeing in Rome proved impossible as the paparazzi continued to be intrusive. Largely cooped up in the hotel, it allowed Eva to see how unhappy her daughter had become; Soraya had forgotten how to smile. The young, happy daughter that Eva remembered at her Swiss school – carefree, full of mischief and practical jokes – had gone. In her second autobiography, Soraya asked, "Was there ever a time when I was completely happy? I have forgotten."

Return to Tehran

Three weeks later, on Monday, 7th September, the situation had stabilised in Iran and Soraya flew to Tehran. She was met by the Shah and his ministers, including many members of the Bakhtiari clan, one of whom was General Teymour, promoted to become the Military Governor of Tehran.

A celebration was given by Zahedi's government at the Saadabad

Palace in October. Soraya noticed that the bows and hand kissing seemed more genuine than previously; families previously indifferent towards her now flattered her. Although seemingly happy to see Soraya return to the social whirl, the Shah took umbrage quickly when he saw Soraya enjoying the exchanges with ministers vying for her attention. The new-found bowing and scraping saddened her, but she admitted that as Empress, she could not show her feelings. She had been plunged back to being Iran's first lady, whether she liked it or not.

She did, however, disclose the duplicity secretly to Dr Ayadi and her aunt, Forough Safar, both of whom the Shah had allowed to be reinstated to the Court; although, at that time, both Nimtaj and Princess Shams were still abroad.

Soraya made Forough her senior lady-in-waiting and appointed a German, Marie-Louise Sägemühl, as her personal secretary. With new-found confidence, and ignoring the Shah's misgivings, she summoned the French decorator, Jansen, to modernise the Echtessassi.

Mosaddeq's Reprieve

Mosaddeq's trial began on Wednesday, 18th November 1953. Fourteen charges were laid against him, including treason. Soraya and the Shah attended the early days of the trial. It gradually became something of a farce, however, as Mosaddeq took over his own defence from his appointed lawyer, continually poking fun at the State's prosecutor and calling him a moron.

On Monday, 21st December, he was found guilty of all the charges and sentenced to death. Soraya, against capital punishment, asked her husband if he would confirm the sentence.

He replied he would not. He explained that without Mosaddeq, their oil would still be in the hands of the British, secretly admitting he respected Mosaddeq's ambitions for Iran.

The Shah commuted his punishment to three years in a prison hospital, followed by indefinite house arrest in his home village of Ahmadabad, near Yazd, south-east of Tehran. Mosaddeq eventually bought the village, grew crops, and founded a primary school and a healthcare centre. He died on Monday, 6th March 1967, aged eighty-five. For most Iranians, Mosaddeq's overthrow demonstrated the duplicity of both the American and British governments. They had presented themselves as defenders of freedom, but did not hesitate to use illegal means to suit their economic interests. It is a sentiment that lingers to this day despite Madeleine Albright, US Secretary of State, apologising for America's wrongdoing in the late 1990s; by then, the Islamic State's intentions towards the West and the US had hardened.

It is a debatable point – if the Shah had accepted Mosaddeq's demands that the Majlis rule and control the military along British lines, leaving the Shah as the constitutional monarch, then would the Pahlavi dynasty have survived? The Shah had managed to scramble back into power, but the calm was only temporary; a stormy sea was to become an uncontrollable tempest that would eventually sink his reign.

Settlement

Soraya and the Shah's fleeing to Rome made front page news all over the world, even as far as South America. The cinema newsreels of them together rekindled interest in Iran's place in the world. The Shah, unlike Mosaddeq, understood that Iran did not have the technical skills to produce oil alone. The Shah agreed that Iran should share the oil profits 50-50 with the British and American companies, known as the 1954 Consortium Agreement. In reality, the share was 45-50, as the Shah personally took 5% of Iran's profits, making him a multibillionaire within months. His share was invested in off-shore banks all over the world.

Relations with the United States and Britain, on the surface, reputedly improved. Indeed, Eisenhower's government immediately gave Tehran a $45 million loan, secured against future oil sales, for immediate social and infrastructure improvements across the country. Called the White Goods Revolution, nationalised industries were set up to produce goods such as cars, washing machines, dish washers, and electric fires. Iranian cars were to be called Paykans. Six thousand were initially imported from Britain's Rootes group's Hillmans to be modified. Within two years, 100,000 per year were being manufactured in Iran. Grants were made available for peasant farmers to purchase their land and for businesses to expand to the extent that foreign competition no longer became a threat.

The improving living standards were being seen as the result of Prime Minister Zahedi, not the Shah. Zahedi, historically a popular hero, known as a decisive leader and with close ties to the US, was seen as the powerhouse. Consequently, a chasm began to open between the Majlis and the Imperial Court. The differences of opinion were sufficient for the Shah to try and capitalise on the split. For example, when opening a new factory, the Shah would try to boost his flagging image by comparing himself with Cyrus the Great. The cold shoulder that the Shah met when visiting America and Britain a year later suggested neither Eisenhower nor Churchill saw him as a reliable, close ally.

Two further years of scheming would be required before the Shah succeeded in removing Zahedi.

15

SORAYA'S POPULARITY PEAKS

Doubts – Revenge or Justice

Having bravely commuted Mosaddeq's sentence against the ruling of the court, the Shah's experience of fleeing to Rome made him less gullible. Feeling his throne was secure, Soraya noticed his self-confidence returned. He continued to listen to his advisers, but unlike previously when he invariably heeded their advice, he tempered their suggestions to make his own decisions. Nonetheless, during the Mosaddeq trial, as fresh evidence of the conspiracy emerged, the Shah was persuaded to appoint a committee to purge former Mosaddeq supporters and members of the Tudeh party. The newly promoted General Teymour Bakhtiar was appointed its chairman. Some years later, the committee became the Shah's secret service, the SAVAK – an abbreviation for the National Organization for Security and Intelligence. Teymour Bakhtiar became its ruthless leader. The committee became notorious for carrying out summary executions. According to Soraya, her husband, as a rule, avoided responsibility by turning a blind eye.

One evening, Soraya found herself in the Echtessassi watching a film with the Shah accompanied by a group of army officers. It depicted civilians being hanged and soldiers being shot by a firing squad. Upset, Soraya left the room. The following morning, she asked the Shah how he could allow such punishments. He answered that the miscreants were traitors who represented a danger to the security of the State, adding that an example had to be made of such men.

Soraya admits in her biography that it reminded her of Reza Shah, who would have acted in the same way. She began worrying if she was always going to have to live under her late father-in-law's ghostly presence.

Wants for Nothing

With the removal of Mosaddeq's threat, the light-hearted atmosphere of the Court returned, despite the Shah's mother and Ashraf returning from exile. Nimtaj quickly resumed looming over her family, but the Shah quietly showed signs of appreciating Soraya's role in supporting him.

With help from Forough and Marie-Louise, Soraya drew up further plans to extensively modernise the Echtessassi. The dark, wooden wall panels were removed and the walls plastered before decorating them in bright, warm colours. Furniture was modernised and the kitchen rebuilt with contemporary units. Carpets were replaced. An indoor swimming pool was built. Soraya's self-esteem grew; she began inviting guests, other than Pahlavis, to her home for afternoon tea. However, the number of dinner parties that Soraya would have liked was restricted by the Shah; he still had qualms about parsimony, except when it was the Pahlavis' birthdays and anniversaries.

Soraya's role as Empress was being accepted by families that had formerly intrigued behind her back. They now vied with each other to pay Soraya compliments. Being shrewd, she used their obsequiousness to her advantage. Already successfully improving the management of the State sanatoriums and the mothers' and children's charities, the Shah entrusted Soraya to additionally supervise the Iranian Red Cross and the Imperial Social Services. In effect, Soraya was in charge of all the welfare organisations in Iran – she was the most powerful woman in Iran.

But in practice, it was not easy. Nimtaj, Ashraf and Shams didn't take kindly to Soraya's increased responsibilities. The three female Pahlavis began to plot; subterfuge was aplenty.

At one of Soraya's unannounced visits to an orphanage, she had been horrified to find filthy children covered with abscesses. They lived in dormitories with neither heat nor hot water; the beds had only a single blanket. There were few toilet facilities. Her inspection of the records revealed many children were kept on the register that had died years earlier. It meant the real mortality rate was higher than the official figures, making the per capita income for the Ministry of Health fraudulently greater. On delving further into the accounts, she was surprised at the scale of corruption. She met nothing but obstacles from the bureaucrats to get something done. She discussed her findings with her husband. She explained she wished to set up a charitable foundation, find unpaid volunteers, and employ doctors whom she could trust. The Shah was sceptical, pointing out the practical difficulties of getting the wealthy to depart with their money. However, he promised his support, underestimating Soraya's determination.

Soraya used her new-found power as Empress. She would shame the high society ladies who were now fawning over her. Initially, small parties of half a dozen were invited to the Echtessassi for tea. She outlined the problem of the children and the elderly living hand by mouth; she asked if they would help.

They could not refuse. She explained she had created a new charity – the Soraya Foundation. She asked them to join for a monthly subscription of thirty US dollars and promise to give up their time;

they agreed unanimously. Nimtaj, Shams and Ashraf had their noses put further out of joint. However, without realising, Soraya's optimistic plans were being built on sand.

The Soraya Foundation

The enthusiastic ladies began by organising a charity ball at the Golestan Palace. Invitations were printed, sold by the ladies to friends, who sold them to other friends. Prizes were given for a tombola. Well-known celebrities from the stage agreed to perform for nothing. The ball was a triumph.

Fundamentals such as coal, blankets and materials to make clothes were bought. The ladies' sewing machines went into overtime while Soraya helped with tacking and hemming. She organised distribution of the outfits to destitute families. Articles in the newspapers were glowing with praise and soon manufacturers were sending beds, more fabrics, and food parcels. Money began arriving – sufficient to rent houses which were converted into hostels. Soraya became by far the most popular person in Iran. All over the country, her name became the most common with new-born girls.

Soraya put the Foundation on a professional footing. She made herself president; the prime minister's wife, Khadijah Zahedi, was made vice-president. Aunt Forough became managing director. Soraya became a roving ambassador, travelling around the country whipping up support from the wives of the landed gentry. Money poured in. Sanatoriums were built in Isfahan, Tabriz, Mashhad and Shiraz. Tehran's new hospital for women and sick children was completed, equipped with the most up-to-date wards and operating theatres.

Soraya was a feminist at heart. She felt strongly about the emancipation of women. She believed Iranian women had been dominated too long by men who treated them as flesh to bear children.

She remembered Adab High School when veiled women, seeing her class in gym clothes, called them she-devils. She was determined girls should have access to playing sports. She decided to create a girls' summer school on the Caspian Sea for gymnastics, swimming, volleyball, and tennis. Opposition was immediate and vocal. Comments such as "unimaginable", "the danger of them sleeping in tents", and "the possibility of sexual harassment" were common.

Soraya's answer was that there would be no danger, as she would be there. The first of many camps opened at Ramsar. Soraya made a roster of senior, trusted supervisors, such as Aunt Forough, Kadijah Zahedi, Iran Bakhtiar, wife of General Teymour Bakhtiar, and others, including herself, who ensured security. Soraya enjoyed playing volleyball and swimming with the girls.

Seeing his wife's success, the Shah allowed her to take over the management of all state-run children's homes. Finding them badly managed, she dismissed the central board of management and personally selected new staff.

Source: Bakhtiari Picture Soraya's Autobiography – Le Palais des Solitude
The first summer camp of the Foundation near Ramsar on the Caspian

Her next project was to set up a publishing house. Classic English, French, German and Greek books were translated into Farsi by volunteers. Printed in huge numbers, the books were sold for no profit. She organised evening literacy classes that were especially popular with older women. Not only was the infant mortality rate dropping, but the literacy figures began rising.

A New-Found Sport

In their spare time, the Shah and Soraya rode their horses, played tennis and volleyball. Each morning, before breakfast, they swam in Echtessassi's indoor pool. They would drive into the Alborz Mountains to ski or go sailing along the shores of the Caspian Sea. However, one evening, while watching an American film, they saw water-skiing – a sport unknown in Iran. They bought a pair of skis from Italy and taught themselves. Once they had the mastered the fundamentals, the Shah bought a new motorboat from Italy and had a private boathouse and pier constructed near Ramsar. Thereafter, it became their chief pastime; both became very proficient.

A Fear of Flying

Soraya makes great play in her biographies that the Shah loved speed, and they often went out in his Mercedes sports car to drive quickly on the desert roads. She claimed in both her biographies that he was a good pilot. However, she gave three incidents that could have proved fatal when he was at the controls. Once on a short flight to Shemiran, he had not checked the weather forecast. They hit a severe storm that had the Shah sweating with fear. On another occasion, when flying to Isfahan, the engine began cutting out and he realised the fuel tanks were empty; he had to use the reserve. Then, when flying the Beechcraft with Prime Minister Zahedi, he needed four attempts to land safely. A description of him as a careless pilot would have been more accurate. Whenever flying with him, Soraya admitted she always breathed a sigh of relief on returning to terra firma.

Iran's Regeneration

While Soraya was working to improve the lot of the children and mothers, the Shah was busy drawing up plans to improve the country's infrastructure. The railway network was enlarged, hydroelectric stations were built and irrigation schemes in the south were extended. By mid-1954, the money was coming from the oil agreements. Iran's 50% of the profits produced a total annual income of over $300 million. The contract with BP, Shell and AMACO would last for twenty-five years.

Farmers and villages retained 50% of their net produce while the remaining sum was ring-fenced to build local schools and hospitals. A large-scale offensive was made against the production of opium. All the poppy fields were destroyed except for a few government-controlled plantations to detoxify addicts and make drugs, such as morphine. The Government financed the official detoxification treatment of over 100,000 addicts. The overall effect of the improvements was Iran's standard of living hit an all-time high.

The Shah encouraged free enterprise with grants to manufacture products previously imported. A new class of industrialists emerged.

Assassination Attempt

Although the country was getting to grips with poverty, in March 1954, two policemen noticed a woman wearing a bourka. Her gait and heavy build intrigued the two officers who approached her and asked for her identification. The person tried to run away but was caught and, on tearing off her veil, they found the individual had a beard. The man turned out to be Dr Fatemi, the man who had announced all Pahlavis should be hanged when Soraya and the Shah were in Rome.

Thought to be dead, there had been a clever ruse engineered by Mosaddeq's followers who had brutally slaughtered an innocent man of similar appearance. Fatemi's bag contained a bomb. He was arrested and admitted he planned to blow-up the Shah. Tried by a military court, he was found guilty of treason and executed by firing squad on 10th November 1954.

Court Formality Relaxed

With the success of Soraya's charitable work, the Shah's regeneration projects, and the increase in oil revenue, the couple lived a much more social life than previously. Whenever they went skiing in the Alborz Mountains or sailing at Ramsar, they invited friends, several of whom were Soraya's Bakhtiari cousins. However, court etiquette remained. At formal functions, if Soraya stood up, everyone stood up and remained standing until she sat down. Soraya admitted this was something she never got used to.

The Shah had noticeably become more relaxed in public. At a masked ball held at Princess Ashraf's home, Soraya told several of her ladies-in-waiting that she would go as Madame de Pompadour, but they were to keep it secret. She then exchanged her outfit with one of her closest friends and attended instead as Joan of Arc. The Shah, in on the ruse, arrived with Soraya's friend. Soraya's dance companions that evening had no idea who she was. Meanwhile, her friend's dance card was full; all her partners thought she was Soraya as they praised her costume and showed her every consideration.

At the end of the evening, Soraya asked her friend what it was like to be an Empress. She replied it was horrible; the men were so respectful!

Order of Chivalry

To recognise Soraya's charitable achievements and increase her prestige, the Shah created a new order of chivalry: the Order of the Pleiades. The decoration was the seven-star constellation, located in the constellation of Taurus, set in precious stones. The order, initially first or second class, could be bestowed by Soraya, as grandmaster of the order, on women of high status from both Iran and abroad whom she considered deserved special recognition. It gave Soraya a status far above her in-laws. Now undisputedly the leading lady in Iran, it didn't go down well with her relations, but they had to accept the status quo. However, resentment continued to fester under the surface.

The Order of the Pleiades

16

THE DARK CLOUD

The Beginning of the End

Soraya and the Shah had been married over three years when the Shah decided that they should be crowned together. The coronation would formalise Soraya as Queen. It proved beyond doubt that his love of Soraya was genuine. However, the constant, overhanging mischief of his mother and twin sister made life difficult.

To prove his sincerity, the Shah wanted a bespoke crown made for Soraya; not an existing one used by his mother and the Qajar dynasty. They went to the National Bank, where the State jewels were kept, to examine the precious stones that could be used. The jewels were not the property of the Shah but belonged to the State. Soraya could not believe her eyes when she saw the mountains of gems for the first time. The Imperial Sceptre, Turkish Janissary swords, and a 1860-carat diamond caught her eye. Soraya noted with some amusement that the bank officials watched their every move. Several hours passed as the couple chose the gems to make the crown, necklace, bracelet, and an Order of the Pleiades imperial broach.

Months passed before the Bank's Board of Governors approved the project. A well-known jeweller, Harry Winston of 5th Avenue,

New York, was chosen to design the pieces. He visited the couple to discuss his ideas. He admitted he had never seen such fabulous gems in all his years as a jeweller. He measured Soraya's neck, arms and forehead before returning to Manhattan with photographs of the precious stones he intended to use to make Soraya's crown and her accessories.

A further six months passed before he returned with the crown and jewellery to supervise the stones being inserted into the settings under the close eye of the bank officials. Everything fitted perfectly, but there was a major problem of an heir.

The Shah had been persuaded by pressure from Nimtaj and Ashraf that his son and heir should be present at the coronation. His naivety in not seeing the trap is, in hindsight, unbelievable. After all, Nimtaj argued, he had been six when he had attended his father and mother's coronation in April 1926. Surely, his heir apparent should attend his? Unable to challenge and deny his mother, he agreed to postpone the event. The unpopularity of his decision among the Court and the general public, when the news seeped out, was to prove a major milestone in his eventual downfall.

Whenever he had broached the subject of an heir with Soraya, the subject had been dropped as it was something that could not be rushed. Soraya's parents had been married six years before she was born. On their own in the evening, the Shah would suggest their first child's Persian names – always a boy. Waiting another year was usually seen as the solution, but Soraya was beginning to think that her only function was to provide the Pahlavis with a male heir. Although the Royal Court remained discreet, Soraya's mother-in-law was not so tactful, taking every opportunity to raise the question in public. She would make malicious remarks along the lines of hoping the forthcoming year would see an increase in the royal household.

The Trip Abroad

In October 1954, the Shah announced that he wished to visit the major political leaders of the western world. His plan was to re-establish personal contacts and improve Iran's international image. Soraya would accompany him. He explained they would be away for three months and that she could buy whatever clothes she required, regardless of expense. Normally parsimonious, his sudden change made her think that he saw her as a sideshow – a glamorous, elegant model.

She ordered her daytime wardrobe from her usual tailor in Tehran but took the Shah at his words and ordered her expensive evening dresses from Paris. They planned to leave in early November, but on 26th October it was the Shah's thirty-fifth birthday. As usual, the whole family gathered that evening for his party at Nimtaj's home. Missing was the Shah's brother, Prince Ali. He was the only person who could succeed to the throne in the event of the Shah's death. Ali had never been late for the Shah's previous birthdays. Ali had planned to fly from his estate on the shores of the Caspian Sea. Everyone became anxious as time wore on and he didn't arrive.

The party finished around midnight, but Ali hadn't arrived. Several phone calls to Ali's staff confirmed that he had departed. The Shah initiated a full-scale search to begin at daylight. It wasn't until five days later that his aircraft was found in the Alborz Mountains. Gloom descended on the Pahlavis. It was now imperative for Soraya to produce a male heir. It was no longer a matter of wait and see. The couple must have a boy – soon.

The departure for America was delayed. In the Court, Nimtaj was telling everyone that Soraya must produce an heir, or else…

The Shah began discussing the matter daily with Soraya trying to persuade her that they must visit the best specialists in New York to see if anything was wrong. Soraya wrote in her autobiography that she no longer felt an Empress, but merely a woman of whom only one thing was expected.

New York

It was a relief for Soraya to fly to the United States on 6th December 1954 to get away from the insinuations and glances of Nimtaj, Ashraf and the Court. She immediately liked New York. They stayed at the Waldorf-Astoria Hotel on 4th Avenue, at the time the world's tallest hotel. She enjoyed strolling down 5th Avenue without being chased by journalists. She loved walking into a shop to be greeted with 'Hello', and on departing, 'Have a nice day'.

On 8th December, the Shah and Soraya entered the Columbia Presbyterian Medical Centre in Manhattan, considered to be the finest hospital in New York. The Shah had decided to have a thorough medical check-up. It had been three years from his peritonitis operation, since when he had not seen a physician. At the hospital, Soraya underwent three days of comprehensive tests: blood and menstruation samples, blood pressure, urine samples, X-rays, and internal examinations. Everything was declared normal. The team of gynaecologists explained to the Shah that all the shocks, upsets and distress that Soraya had endured over the previous three years could be the cause of her failure to conceive. He was assured everything would, in time, return to normal.

After leaving hospital, their personal guide, Fleur Cowles, whom they had previously met in Tehran, purchased theatre tickets, took them around the museums, accompanied them up the Empire State Building and showed them Central Park. She gave several parties at her own home and arranged for them to have lunch with the mayor, Robert Wagner Jr. With high hopes for a productive future, Soraya and the Shah flew to Washington to stay at the Persian Embassy.

Washington

President Eisenhower and his wife greeted the couple on the steps of the White House. There followed the usual reception in the drawing room, meeting endless people, followed by a formal lunch. To Soraya's relief, Mamie Eisenhower, possibly seeing Soraya tiring after lunch, took her on a private tour of the White House, including her own quarters. She showed her the portraits of the past presidents, painted by the great American artists, and impressed Soraya with her knowledge of American history. They compared Iranian and American dishes in the kitchens where Mamie appeared to know the names of all the staff.

That evening, they were left to their own devices and it became clear that the American Government had made no entertainment arrangements for their four-day visit to the capital. Apart from Fleur Cowles and Iranian officials, they knew no one in America. The Shah and Soraya were expected to remain unattended. Fortunately, the Persian ambassador was quickly able to employ a public relations agent for the rest of their time in the United States. The following day, a reception was held at the embassy for local dignitaries who had probably paid a fortune to the PR agent. Moreover, accompanied trips with expert guides were quickly arranged to Arlington Cemetery, George Washington's house at Mount Vernon, the three museums of natural history, aerospace, and Gallery of Art, as well as the Jefferson and Lincoln memorials.

California

Soraya's Skye terrier, Tony, who was accompanying them, had been a problem. In New York he had nipped the ankle of an elevator attendant, but at their hotel in San Francisco he attacked a waiter bringing up their breakfast. Consequently, a vet was required to vaccinate the waiter against rabies and a claim for damages was made. Thus, Tony became the most expensive member of their retinue. The terrier had to be sent back to stay with Eva in Cologne. As a result, Soraya's love of dogs was given much publicity; for the rest of the tour, well-wishers kept offering her dogs.

Their PR agent earned his fees on the West Coast. Their first introduction was to George Hearst, the son of the newspaper tycoon portrayed in the film *Citizen Kane*. He invited them to stay for Christmas at his castle, San Simeon, south of San Francisco. There Soraya slept in the bed of Madame du Barry, Louis XV's mistress.

Los Angeles

In Hollywood, they visited the sets of Cecil B de Mille and discovered snobbery was rife among actors. Ironically, this stood them in good stead as the Shah was seen as a King and Soraya as his Queen. Having played kings and queens in their make-believe world, the actors felt honoured to mix with real ones. Greer Garson entertained them to lunch and showed them her new home where, in the bathroom, marble steps led down to a sunken bath. The scale and opulence was greater than anything Soraya had seen before. At a reception, they met Barbara Stanwyck, Judy Garland and Kim Novak. Soraya was delighted to meet her childhood flame, Robert Taylor. Admitting to him that she had had a teenage crush on him, he reputedly replied it was a pity that they hadn't met earlier.

Seen as suitable to meet the Shah and Soraya privately for dinner, possibly because they had been married for twenty-one years, were Gary Cooper and his wife Veronica. The two couples clicked, enjoying each other's company so much that they met a few days later to ski together in Sun Valley, Idaho, where the Coopers had a winter retreat.

The evening was spent playing bridge. Soraya described Gary as a very quiet, shy man who spoke little.

Florida

They flew to Miami where their PR agent had arranged for Charles Wrightsman, an oil magnate and onetime President of Standard Oil, to offer Soraya and the Shah his hospitality. Wrightsman's private aircraft met them at Miami airport and took them to Palm Beach. There, his estate, according to Soraya, outshone anything they had seen in America.

They met Allen Dulles, the Head of the Central Intelligence Agency. He played bridge with the couple and Soraya described him as a charming man who enjoyed showing them photos of his grandchildren. The Shah thanked him for helping to overthrow Mosaddeq, but Soraya was never present when the pair held private discussions. After a few days relaxing, Wrightsman gave a party in their honour. A young senator turned up with his wife, Jack and Jacqueline Kennedy. The two couples, the youngest guests staying at the villa, hit it off immediately and would remain friends until Kennedy's assassination in November eight years later. On leaving, Wrightsman gave Soraya two small Tibetan terriers.

17

EUROPE

England

On 15th February 1955, the Shah and Soraya sailed from New York aboard the Queen Mary to Southampton. The Shah was apprehensive about how the English would receive him after the AIOC's oil deal. The AIOC, renamed British Petroleum (BP), was effectively state-

Courtesy Getty Images
Buckingham Palace with the Queen and Prince Philip

owned. The Shah confided with Soraya that he thought they might get a frosty reception and that he was relying on her to smooth the path.

They were met at Victoria Railway Station in London by the Duke of Gloucester and the following day met the Queen at Buckingham Palace. Diplomatically in her biography, Soraya described Queen Elizabeth as "maintaining a certain reserve", as if having "an invisible wall around her". Queen Elizabeth showed neither Soraya nor the Shah much affection. Her conversation was "always correct, as though her words were chosen carefully". The fact that the Shah was dressed most inappropriately in his Air Marshal's uniform may have upset the Queen, as she was a known stickler for correct dress. Nothing political was mentioned and conversation over dinner was somewhat stilted until the Queen discovered a common interest with the Shah – the breeding of horses. By contrast, throughout the evening Prince Philip was "friendly". His chatter with Soraya was "animated and witty". At the end of the meal, Prince Charles and his sister, Princess Anne, appeared to say hello. Their bows, curtsies, and furtive looks at each other charmed the Shah. He raised his eyes to Soraya and she knew what he was thinking.

The following day, they took afternoon tea with the Queen Mother, who was described by Soraya as warm and friendly.

The Queen Mother impressed the Shah with her knowledge of Persian history, particularly the period of Darius and Xerxes. She discussed with him Darius's Royal Highway from Persepolis to Lydia in modern Turkey, and the battles of Marathon and Thermopylae.

Above all, Soraya wanted to meet Churchill as she had read his memoir, *My Early Life*, which included a chapter on Iran. Churchill was still Prime Minister but was in ill-health and would resign two months later. The couple's itinerary included a working lunch at his home, Chartwell, in SE England. Unfortunately, Churchill had acquired a new hearing aid and throughout the meal he kept taking it off and putting it back on. Finally, he stuffed it, unceremoniously, in his pocket, declaring loudly that he could live without it. When they discussed Persian politics, he grew discourteous and grumpier. He was rude, despite the fact that he must have known Iran was about to join the Baghdad Pact (CENTO) a few weeks later. They were both glad to leave, feeling exhausted and disappointed. However, Soraya had mentioned to him that she was fond of dogs, had a Skye terrier, and had been given two Tibetan terriers in Florida. Within hours of returning to the Iranian Embassy, a bulldog arrived courtesy of the great man. A suggestion was made to call him Winston, but fearing it might be taken the wrong way, Soraya settled on Boris.

Courtesy Alamy images

Soraya leaving Churchill after an unsatisfactory lunch.

West Germany

The couple's first stop was Hamburg, where they were given an overwhelmingly warm reception. Despite the snow, the road to their hotel was lined with well-wishers cheering and waving. Their visit had been given a great deal of publicity as everyone knew Soraya's mother was German. At the hotel, an enormous crowd had gathered beneath the couple's window. They shouted over and over for Soraya to appear on the balcony. She opened the curtains and waved, but the volume increased.

The Shah ordered her to open the windows and stand on the balcony. His jaw was set, his look cruelly harsh.

Soraya realised he resented her getting all the attention. The crowd were shouting in German, 'Soraya komn heraus ganz Munchen seht vor deinnem Haus!' Soraya understood the ovation, but the Shah didn't. His wife receiving all the cheering was not going down well with him.

The following morning, she had her hair trimmed by the hotel's hairdresser. She was to discover later that the hairdresser had sold several of her locks to admirers.

At Dusseldorf, the reception was equally rapturous. After dinner a crowd of several thousand again gathered outside their hotel bedroom and would not leave. Soraya had gone to bed, but her husband insisted she put a coat over her nightdress and appear on the balcony. It was a decision she would regret a few days later.

Their official state visit was to Bonn, where they were greeted by both President Heuss and Chancellor Adenauer at the airport. German receptions were more formal and bureaucratic than in either the USA or England. On each evening occasion, she wore one of her Parisian dresses, with her imperial sash.

At Cologne, Soraya's Skye terrier that had been staying with Eva met the two Tibetan terriers. All-out war ensued with one of the Tibetan dogs running away into nearby woods where the snow was knee deep. The local radio station was alerted and hundreds of volunteers set out to help the search. Two days later, the dog returned. Admirers wanted to give Soraya more dogs, which she had to refuse, although eventually she was persuaded to keep a miniature pinscher and the Shah kept a trained police dog.

At Baden-Baden, they stayed with an old friend of the Shah's from his days at school in Switzerland. Their last stop was Munich, where the crowds were greater than ever. Having felt unwell for several days, she came down with flu, which she attributed to her balcony appearances in Hamburg and Dusseldorf. Although running a high temperature and with the local doctor wanting her to spend three or four days in bed, she refused. Injected with penicillin, she completed their official engagements before flying to Baghdad.

At Baghdad, the Shah wished to discuss with King Faisal, what he called private matters. Soraya flew on to Tehran to a warm welcome from Prime Minister Zahedi. Their tour, with Soraya as the undisputed star, had been seen as a great success in the Iranian press.

The Shah's Paranoia

A few weeks after returning from their overseas tour, in early April, Soraya was lunching with the Shah at Echtessassi. She instinctively knew something was on his mind and asked what was worrying him. He confessed that he believed Zahedi was not to be trusted and would have to go. He no longer believed Zahedi was making serious attempts to eliminate corruption and nepotism. He claimed many members of Zahedi's family had been given well-paid public appointments, his ministers were accepting bribes, and Zahedi's bank account was suspiciously healthy.

Soraya was appalled, thinking how her husband could dismiss

the very man who had saved the monarchy. Her protest was ignored. She was puzzled how the Shah knew details of Zahedi's bank account. It led her to remember the Shah having several private meetings with Alan Dulles when they were in Florida. At the time, the Shah's dealings with the Head of the CIA had meant nothing, but now she started to speculate if her husband had a private team spying on his own government officials.

Trying to excuse his behaviour, she wondered if he was worried about Zahedi's increasing popularity, possibly afraid Zahedi could topple him. As far as she knew, there was no evidence of a plot, but Middle East politics were full of cases where reigning dynasties had been replaced by politicians. The Caliph, Mehmed VI, in Turkey, King Farouk in Egypt, even her husband's father had proved to be susceptible. Soraya began to believe the Shah was suffering from paranoia.

A day or two later, Soraya was taking coffee after lunch with the Shah, when Zahedi arrived.

The Shah greeted him warmly, as if nothing was the matter. When Zahedi had settled, the Shah thanked him for all he had done. He then tossed a fast ball, telling him that he thought the responsibilities of State had become too much for him.

Zahedi went pale as the Shah suggested Zahedi should represent Iran at the United Nations in Geneva, with a handsome salary and a free house. General Zahedi, their saviour from Mosaddeq, accepted his dismissal and retired to Switzerland. He never returned to Iran. The Shah's strongest supporter in the Majlis had gone and Soraya asked herself whether Zahedi had upset the Shah's mother. Only Nimtaj could have exerted so much pressure on her son to incite such irrational behaviour. Zahedi died in Geneva in September 1963, aged seventy-one. The unforgivable, groundless dismissal of the most popular politician was to be a huge nail in the Shah's coffin.

Royal Matchmaker

Some months later, as the summer approached, the Shah finally confided to Soraya what he had discussed with King Faisal in Baghdad after their world trip. The Shah had offered the hand of his daughter, Shahnaz, to the king in marriage. He explained the unification of the two dynasties would ensure a great future for their countries. Soraya said nothing but remembered the Shah's own disastrous arranged marriage, as well as those of his sisters, and wondered what was coming next.

He explained King Faisal was keen on the idea and would like to meet his daughter. Then, to Soraya's amazement, he asked her to arrange for Shahnaz to meet the King when he would be on his yacht in the South of France later that summer. Soraya reluctantly agreed. However, she made it crystal clear that she would exert no influence on Shahnaz, who must be free to choose her own husband.

Anticipating Soraya's lack of enthusiasm, the Shah suggested a second choice – Aly Salman Khan, the son of the aging Aga Khan III. Aly Khan had recently divorced his second wife, the actress Rita Hayworth, and was forty-four. He even had a son, Karim, who was five years older than Shahnaz. The Aga Khan had led the Shah to believe that if Aly married Shahnaz, then he would make Aly his successor.

The Shah instructed Soraya that as Aly Khan would be in the South of France at the same time, he wanted her to arrange both potential suitors to meet Shanaz.

Soraya was furious at having to undertake the matchmaking, as she felt she had no right to determine the fate of an innocent fifteen-year-old. The Shah had arranged for Princess Shams to escort Shahnaz from her Swiss boarding school to the Hotel du Cap in Antibes where they would meet Soraya, who would have arrived two days earlier.

Soraya went to dinner the evening before Shams and Shahnaz arrived with the Aga Khan at his villa in Cannes. Ironically, without knowing Soraya's mission, both the twenty-year-old Faisal and Aly Khan were present. The following day, the two princesses arrived. Soraya had organised a lunch for Shanaz to meet Aly Khan and King Faisal. In her biography, Soraya described Shahnaz as polite but coldly withdrawn.

Thinking the problem was that they were shy in each other's presence, Soraya arranged a second meeting at a less formal setting in old Antibes. The dinner was a disaster, as the three hardly spoke to each other. Indeed, Aly Khan showed more interest in Soraya; unsurprising, as his playboy reputation with married women was second to none. Due to his well-publicized affairs, Aly Khan was mentioned in a verse of Noel Coward's 1950s lyrics for Cole Porter's 1928 song *Let's Do It, Let's Fall in Love*. Shahnaz later confided to Soraya that she didn't like King Faisal at all.

The matchmaking fiasco was to turn out well for Shahnaz, as King Faisal was assassinated in a revolution led by General Karim Qasim three years later on 14th July 1958, when the Kingdom of Iraq became a republic.

Aly Khan never took over from his father. Aly's son became Aga Khan IV when his grandfather died in July 1957.

18

THE JEWEL IN THE CROWN

India

The year 1955 passed and there was no sign of an heir. Numerous visits to specialists in Switzerland produced the familiar diagnosis that there was nothing wrong. In desperation, remedies such as diets, injections and countless vitamin pills were tried. The advice to be patient and everything will be all right wore thin with Soraya, as well as with her in-laws. Unknown to Soraya, Ashraf had started to bring attractive girls, whether married or not, to Court to be introduced to her brother. The Shah's closest advisers, Ernest Peron and Asadollah Alam, were aware of what Ashraf, with her mother's connivance, was plotting. A new wife had to be found at any cost. Their inclusion in the conspiracy would lead to what Soraya, much later, would describe to her cousin as, "The Royal Court became a dirty swamp of black mud".

In February 1956, another overseas trip was arranged for the Shah to consolidate his position as Head of State. In the era of the Cold War, independent India leaned towards the Soviet Union, whereas

Iran's position in CENTO, together with its other members: Pakistan, Iraq, Turkey and the UK, were pro-American. The absence of the US in the Baghdad Pact was explained by a pro-Israel lobby in the American Senate, according to a leak from the US Secretary of State, Foster Dulles.

Seeing his country as a link between East and West, the Shah's state visit to India was designed to strengthen his position by bridging the gap. Soraya saw it as pushing in time before their marriage inevitably broke up. The Shah was sufficiently canny to realise the world's press would give the trip little publicity without showing off his jewel in the crown; he seemed contented for Soraya to take the limelight. After three days of formal talks in Delhi, there followed three weeks of travelling around the Indian sub-continent.

Everywhere, the crowds flocked to see the Queen of Iran, rather than the King. Mostly, the couple were guests of maharajas from historic Islamic states that had been absorbed into India, rather than Pakistan.

The first visit was to meet the Maharaja of Mysore, Jayachamarendra Wadiyar. He had ruled from 1940 until the Indian monarchies were abolished in 1950. Thereafter, maharajas retained their titles as honorary heads of their former royal families. Jayacham had married twice. With his first wife, Satya, he had no children, but with his second, Tripura, he fathered six. If Soraya noticed the irony, no mention is made in her biographies.

Jayacham, a keen sportsman, was a good tennis player and sponsored Raman Krishnan to participate at Wimbledon and paid for the off-spin bowler Prasanna to tour the West Indies with India's cricket team.

Jayacham was also a connoisseur of classical music. Aspirations to become a concert pianist were cut short by the untimely death of his father. He gave £10,000 pounds a year for three years to put the Philharmonia Orchestra on a firm financial base, allowing it to engage Herbert von Karajan as its conductor.

Despite Jayacham being a philanthropist of the arts, music and sport, Soraya was surprised when, at a banquet, she and her two ladies-in-waiting were the only ladies present in the banqueting hall with over one hundred men. When she queried the absence of ladies, the Maharaja calmly explained that the women, including his mother and two wives, were sitting in the balcony watching them behind net curtains. He added that it was customary practice that when women were being driven in cars they had to remain hidden behind curtains.

On another visit, they met the Nizam of Hyderabad. Supposedly, he was the richest man in the world. A renowned benevolent ruler, he patronized education, science, and infrastructure projects such as damns, electric power stations and railways. Soraya commented in her second biography that she saw little evidence of his wealth. As he grew older, he had become a renowned miser. He wore a badly frayed, forty-year-old fez. An apocryphal tale was that he sent a servant to buy a new blanket and gave him 35 rupees. When he returned, the servant explained the cheapest was 45 rupees. Nizam apparently replied that he would do without.

Nonetheless, in WWI he donated sufficient funds to the war effort to equip a new RAF Squadron, No. 110 Sqn, with De Havilland bombers. The Squadron was named the Hyderabad Sqn. It was eventually disbanded in 1971 at RAF Changi, Singapore, when equipped with Whirlwind Helicopters.

As he grew older, he became evermore eccentric. His hands-off approach to managing his affairs led to him being swindled by his financial advisers. In 1972, he bought a half-million-acre sheep station in Western Australia where he spent most of his final years.

Soraya was surprised to find the poverty in India worse than Iran. Wherever they went, the servants were poorly dressed and often so thin she could count their ribs. She couldn't get over seeing cows being better fed than the peasants or monkeys being treated as gods.

Turkey

In March 1956, the couple went to Turkey for an official visit. The president, Celâl Bayar, met them informally on his yacht. After dinner, they played cards in the evening. The following day, when the Shah was reviewing a military parade, an officer, appointed to be her consort for the afternoon, asked Soraya if she would like a trip in a submarine. Thinking he was joking, she accepted the offer and found herself, with her two ladies-in-waiting, being driven to a military naval base near Istanbul. A small craft ferried them out to a moored submarine. After disembarking from the small tender, and clambering aboard, they climbed down the narrow steel ladder into the bowels of the boat. After a twenty-minute trip, at a depth of 120 feet, one of Soraya's attendants fainted and the trip had to be curtailed, but not before the captain had explained all the boat's controls, its navigation system, and allowed Soraya to up-periscope. She thoroughly enjoyed the experience with the friendly, relaxed, crew. For Soraya, it was the highlight of her visit to Turkey. Later that evening, when she told the Shah of her trip, he went green with envy.

King Saud

Shortly after returning from Turkey, in April 1956, the King of Saudi Arabia, Ibn Saud, arrived with an entourage of seventy, all male, officials. The plan was to entertain him with an evening garden party at Saadabad, but the question arose as to whether women guests should be invited. The King was a Wahhābī Sunni, an ultraconservative sect that practiced strict Sharia Law whereby women were kept separate in public. After some discussion with the Shah's advisers, it was decided that as women in Iran attended such functions, an exception would not be made. In the event, the King seemed delighted with the presence of women and spent a long time conversing with Soraya in Arabic through an interpreter.

Alcoholic drinks were absent at the tables, but Soraya had arranged for a small bar to be erected behind a copse at the bottom of the garden. The international diplomats had sufficient nous to slip away occasionally without being seen. However, as darkness came, the glow of their cigarettes could be seen through the bushes. Soraya, when asked by the King what the lights were, replied quickly they were fireflies.

Soviet Union

In June 1956, the couple went to the Soviet Union. It was the first visit by any of the world's royal families to the USSR since 1913. Their suite in the Kremlin was extensive. It consisted of several reception rooms, a dining room furnished in dark, oak furniture, and two en-suite bedrooms. Wherever they went, from a steel factory to the opera, Soraya couldn't get over the quantities of food and drink put in front of them. Whenever accompanied by Khrushchev, he would press Soraya to eat more as if he thought she was too slim. Aware that her mother, Eva, had been born in Moscow, and somehow knowing Soraya had been taught Russian when young, he constantly paid her compliments in Russian, using phrases such as telling her how beautiful she looked. She found this amusing, as the Soviet Government hadn't appeared to have done much to improve the lot of Russian women. Their clothes were drab and made of poor material, their hair was unwashed and ill-kempt, and they tended to be frumpy due to poor diets. Soraya had noticed, when travelling around Moscow, the lack of variety of vegetables in the market.

At Mrs Khrushchev's tea party, held at her home exclusively for Moscow's professional ladies, there was no elegance. Soraya wondered if striking a note of femininity was considered contrary to the teachings of the Soviet revolution.

They visited Stalingrad, Leningrad, Tashkent, and Kiev. The large crowds were always friendly. Subsequently, Soraya received many affectionate letters and telegrams from unknown people asking if they could name their next girl Soraya.

Throughout the whole tour, they were watched by the secret police, usually disguised as servants. Forewarned, the Shah and Soraya were careful that their private conversations were not overheard. However, one evening, alone in their suite of rooms, Soraya casually remarked that she would have liked to have seen the Bolshoi Ballet. Two hours later, an official arrived and asked if they would like him to arrange an evening at the ballet. A few days later, she sat next to Khrushchev and they conversed in Russian about the ballet, *Swan Lake*. Soraya admits in her second autobiography that her Russian improved immensely during their tour.

On another occasion, the Shah had been to an air display and seen a small aircraft that he thought would suit his purposes for flying around Iran. He casually mentioned this to Soraya when they were getting into bed. Soraya told him to forget the idea as the price would be extortionate.

When they returned to Iran, the Shah found a new light plane was waiting for him at Tehran airport.

19

THE DIVORCE

The Slow Build-up Accelerates

Soraya's first possible inkling of her value to the Shah had begun when they had been preparing to visit the United States. By then, they had been married two and a half years. His decision to have a medical check-up in New York and his casual suggestion that Soraya should also be checked over had irritated her. She went along with the idea, consoling herself that her mother had been married six years before giving birth.

She knew the international gossip columns forever speculated about an imminent heir. Whenever she had gone abroad, the magazines claimed it was to see a gynaecologist. At Court, no one mentioned the subject. The only exception who dared to raise the subject was the Shah's mother.

Until the fall of Mosaddeq, the subject of a male heir had not cropped up in the Iranian newspapers. However, as Soraya's successful achievements multiplied, her popularity mushroomed. The work of her foundation was bearing fruit. Hostels and hospitals were being built, children were being fed, rickets and TB were in decline, and girls were being educated. As news of the affection shown to her on her visits abroad reached home, questions of succession began in the Iranian press. Soraya had become a model ambassador who had improved the world's image of Iran. The whole world was waiting for Soraya to give birth to the crown prince. But for her Pahlavi mother-in-law from hell, it wasn't enough.

Whispers

February 1957 saw the couple's sixth wedding anniversary. Soraya had been born on her mother's sixth wedding anniversary. The significance of the date had neither gone unnoticed by Soraya nor the Pahlavis. Since returning from Russia, Soraya had very slowly become depressed as she realised she may be reaching the end of her usefulness. She began imagining groups of courtiers whispering behind her back; their downcast smiles suggested they knew her position was becoming fragile. She noticed the Shah spending more time away on business. He was often absent for two or three nights. His explanation was that the far-flung regiments he was inspecting always held a dining-in night afterwards, which would last into the early hours. However, at the beginning of their marriage, the Shah would always have flown home to be with her. His excuse was wearing thin, but she reluctantly accepted his periodic absences as part of her job.

Soraya tried to console herself by knowing she had improved the world's image of Iran during their overseas trips but was aggrieved that the only people showing open, genuine affection toward her were those who had worked with her in the Soraya Foundation. Her volunteers knew children no longer went hungry and were better educated. Women's lot had improved, and the sick were receiving superior medical attention.

However, those women, who could afford to read the illustrated magazines from Paris and Rome, were aware of the alarm within the Pahlavis. Not every journal hinted the problem was with Soraya. One international periodical speculated the attempt on the Shah's life in 1949 had traumatized him to the extent that he had become sterile.

The Shah and Soraya avoided discussing the subject for fear of hurting each other.

Madame Claude

The Diary of Asadollah Alam, Volume 5, one of a series of seven volumes published posthumously, claimed that the Shah had an insatiable appetite for sex. The memoirs are exceptionally detailed documents of the life and deeds of the Shah as seen by Alam, arguably the Shah's closest ally and friend.

Exactly when Alam, Peron and Ashraf had started to procure girls to entertain the Shah from the infamous Parisian Madame Claude, real name Fernande Grudet, is uncertain. Soraya's cousin was vague when I asked her but thought it was soon after the couple's return from Russia. With the cooperation of the manager of Iran Air at Paris Orly Airport, girls began being flown to Tehran on a regular basis. The joke, passing around Iranian upper society, according to Soraya's cousin, was that the imperial title of "Adjutant to his Majesty" was being handed out to pimps. Before being introduced to the Shah, the girls had to be examined medically and sign a non-disclosure agreement and keep their visit secret. It was only after her divorce that Soraya learnt the truth about her husband's periods of absence.

In her biography, titled *Madame*, Madame Claude claimed she had been a member of the French Resistance during the war and had been imprisoned in a Nazi concentration camp. Afterwards, she worked as a prostitute, but in the early fifties, she went into management. She eventually set up the most exclusive prostitution network in Europe.

A witty quotation from her biography is, *Men pay money for two reasons: food and sex. I wasn't much of a cook.*

Besides the Shah, her wealthy clientele reputedly included politicians such as John F Kennedy, Charles de Gaulle, Georges Pompidou, and Colonel Gadhafi. Film stars included Marlon Brando and Rex Harrison. Eventually imprisoned for tax evasion, she died in Nice in December 2015, aged ninety-two.

Ultimatum

In April 1957, the Shah, dissatisfied with the progress of rooting out corruption by Prime Minister Hussein Ala's government, appointed Manouchehr Eghbal as his replacement. Eghbal, a doctor of medicine, had been educated at the Sorbonne in Paris and married a Frenchwoman. He had formerly been Minister of Health. A few days after his appointment, he had an audience with the Shah. Eghbal made it clear that he would not serve unless the question of an heir was resolved.

There can be little doubt that had the couple been alone in the world, then there may have been no limit to their patience. They had learned to understand and support each other, growing closer as they worked to improve the country's standard of living. Soraya had shared their political crises in a way no one else, including his sisters and mother, could. Although she wanted to continue her charity work, where she had extensive plans for the future, she began to realise it was not enough. After what felt like an endless procession of doctors, white coats, internal inspections, pills, tests and differing advice, she'd had enough.

She felt she had earned her position as Iran's first lady, the right to be Empress of Iran. But it wasn't enough. She knew she had failed in her primary function to bear children, and decided not to shilly-shally.

She began thinking of what she had missed from her youth. Seven years had passed where girls, with whom she had been at school, had been having fun: dancing, laughing, going places without bodyguards, and driving cars unescorted by police cars. She had never enjoyed freedom to do what she wanted. Gritting her teeth, she decided to take the bull by the horns.

Soraya Resolute

In July 1957, the Shah and Soraya were walking alone in the grounds of the Saadabad Palace when Soraya broached the subject of succession. She told the Shah she could persevere no longer. She didn't want to be seen responsible that if something happened to the Shah, there would be no heir and resulting chaos in the country.

Surprised by her openness, he asked what she would suggest. Her reply stunned him when she insisted his eldest half-bother, Gholam, must become his heir.

He explained that it would be contrary to the constitution, drawn up by his father, which stipulated that the children of Reza Shah's third and fourth wives could not inherit. After a long pause, he added that the Council of Elders would never agree to change the constitution.

Soraya had never heard of the Council. Doubting if it existed, she asked herself if this was his latest ploy to sit on the fence and do nothing.

She decided to test him. She challenged him to summon the Council. He shook his head. Looking at the ground, he replied they would never agree. She saw something that she had suspected for a long time. Her husband was not only a ditherer but prepared to lie when it suited him.

She realised he was weak and afraid to pit himself against his mighty father's laws. Frustrated, she blurted out that they must separate permanently.

His eyes welled-up as they walked on. There was no question that he loved Soraya, but he was torn between his wife and his country. Many minutes of silence passed before he suggested he could take a "sigheh". Within Islam-Shia law, men can marry a woman, called a sigheh. It is a temporary marriage that can last from a few hours to a lifetime. He explained that his sigheh marriage could last until she had given birth to a male child, Then he would divorce her. In this way, Soraya would remain at his side as Empress.

It was the straw that broke the camel's back. Her reaction was violent; she went into a rage. Rejecting the proposal out of hand, she realised he wanted it both ways. She screamed at him, asking what right had he to take as many wives as he wanted, but she, as Empress, could only have one husband. She turned away, swearing he was pathetic.

The Shah ran after her, trying to pacify her. He pointed out that his mother had allowed his father to take a third and fourth wife, but Nimtaj had remained Empress. Soraya's angry retort was that times had changed and pointed out that his father hadn't chosen his mother to take to South Africa. She would not discuss the idea any further. Soraya describes in her biography how the Sword of Damocles that had hung over them for four years had finally fallen.

Weeks followed; their relationship was strained to the point that they slept in different bedrooms. The Shah claimed he was making moves for the Council of Elders to consider a change in the constitution to allow his half-brother replace him. Soraya didn't believe him. Their relationship hit rock bottom when he told Soraya that under no circumstances was it to be thought he was driving her out of the country. It was a feeble attempt to pass the blame for a divorce onto Soraya. Somehow, despite their attempt to keep their quarrel secret, rumors were soon leaking around the Court, presumably initiated by the Shah's so-called advisers. Neither the Shah's family nor Soraya's parents let on they were aware of what was happening. However, both sides knew the marriage was finished.

Soraya admitted she was broken. She felt she had failed, despite her efforts to be a successful empress. In preparation for the day she would leave Iran, Soraya began making plans. Her German PPS, Fräulein Sägemühl, had secretly begun sorting the photos of the past years, along with hundreds of letters and documents. She was burning those considered unimportant. Personal items were separated between those Soraya could take with her to Europe from those that would have to be sent on when she left Tehran.

In January 1958, the push came to the shove. The Shah encouraged Soraya to go skiing at St Moritz. He wanted to give the world the impression that their relationship was sound and Soraya was simply taking a holiday with her mother. He promised to ring Soraya daily and keep her up to date with developments. They even agreed a simple code, knowing their conversations would be getting overheard. Accompanying her to Switzerland were her PPS and Marshal of the Court, General Yazdan-Panah, with his wife.

The End of the Fairy Tale

On 13th February 1958, only one day after her seventh wedding anniversary, Soraya left Tehran for the last time. She stayed at The Palace Hotel where her mother and brother, Bijan, joined her. The hotel was full of acquaintances showering her with invitations to après ski parties. Despite feeling miserable, she learnt to smile, thereby concealing the truth from every one.

On the first day, she waited for a phone call, but nothing happened, neither on the second, nor the third. Impatient, she rang Tehran to ask the Shah what was happening. She knew what his answer would be: his half-brothers weren't seen as suitable. The constitution could not be changed. She said a simple, 'Goodbye' – the last word she ever spoke to her husband – and put the phone down. She decided to confide with her mother, who offered caution and suggested they consult with General Panah. In the event, his eyes welled up and, trembling with emotion, he was speechless. He had had no inkling of the problem, and had never heard of the Council.

Eva and Soraya decided to stay until their hotel booking finished so as not to arouse suspicions. On 22nd February, fate intervened; Soraya's father rang from Cologne to say he had broken his ankle. They packed their bags and left for Germany with Soraya's secretary. General Panah and his wife returned to Tehran. Soraya was looking forward to the privacy of her parent's home.

Eva and Soraya arrived to find her father stretched out on his bed with his leg in plaster. She nervously told him that her marriage was over and she was getting divorced. Expecting him to be angry, she was relieved when he hugged her and whispered, 'Thank God!' They remained in an embrace for what seemed ages, both weeping tears of happiness. It was a major turning point in their hitherto somewhat distant relationship.

The Forlorn Hope Delegation

Three days later, Dr Ayadi and General Yazdan-Panah arrived in Cologne to plead with Soraya. They told Eva their mission was to explain to Soraya how the government could not change the constitution. They wished to enlighten Soraya that after weeks of debate, the verdict to retain the status quo had been close-run. Eva, knowing the fiction of the Council, remained firm with them. Dr Ayadi described himself and the General as the last chance of reconciliation and pleaded to meet Soraya. Eva replied firmly that Soraya had locked herself in her bedroom and would not come out. Soraya, she explained, felt enough was enough and returning to Tehran would achieve nothing.

The pair flew back to Tehran empty-handed. On hearing Soraya's rejection, the Shah insisted General Panah immediately return to plead with Soraya again. When she refused to meet him, it was finally all over. Soraya's cousin, the General's daughter-in-law, confirmed this second visit did occur.

On 21st March 1958, Iranian New Year's Day, an apparently disconsolate Shah announced on radio that he was divorcing Soraya. He claimed he was doing it unwillingly as he had a duty to the people of Iran to give them a son. Astonishingly, the Shah had a statement prepared by his staff, probably Peron or Alam, for Soraya to read in reply. In it, she was to admit that she had longed for the split for some time.

However, she was not prepared to ease his conscience. Instead, she issued her own statement conveying her deepest regret, explaining that for the future of the Iranian State she was sacrificing her own happiness and consenting to the permanent separation from the Shah.

The curtain had fallen on the fairy-tale. A few days later, Soraya received a letter from the Shah regretting all that had happened. She never replied.

On hearing the news, the people of Iran showed their sorrow. Pictures of Soraya were sold in shops throughout the country. The masses gathered in the market squares, holding up the pictures, pleading for her to return. The women involved with Soraya's charitable work organised a protest; the Shah forbade it. Others publicly declared they would no longer attend functions at Court. The Shah, believing he was appointed by God to rule, did not understand the strong feelings of his people for their queen. Attempting to publicly blame Soraya for the divorce was a major blunder, as his subjects saw through him. In their eyes, his ploy confirmed he was untrustworthy.

Similar crucial errors in the future would accumulate to ensure his downfall. His plummet from grace had begun.

All over the world, every newspaper showed pictures of Soraya. Despite the arrogance of the Shah's statement, the entire world's press made it clear where their sympathies lay.

The headline-making divorce inspired French songwriter Françoise Mallet-Joris to write a poem that later became a hit pop-song, *"Je Veux Pleurer Comme Soraya"* – I want to cry like Soraya.

Princess Gabriella of Savoy

In February 1959, the Shah showed his fickleness. He indicated his interest to a journalist of marrying Princess Maria Gabriella of Savoy, the second daughter of the deposed King Umberto II of Italy. An editorial about the rumors surrounding the marriage in the Vatican newspaper, *L'Osservatore Romano*, claimed that Pope John XXIII considered the match of a Muslim sovereign to a Catholic princess impossible as, under Canon Law, a Roman Catholic who married a divorced person would be automatically excommunicated. When the news leaked out, his action poured petrol on the fire. Iranian masses wanted to know how a Muslim Shah could wish to marry a Roman Catholic.

20

RUMOURS AND FALSEHOODS

So-called Impeccable Sources

The stream of news that all was not well within the Court of Iran had been seeping out for years, but in late July 1957, the leaks in the damn burst. Whether an unscrupulous servant had witnessed the Saadabad altercation is unknown, but within days a torrent of rumours quickly flooded the international papers. Headlines such as *Will Shah's Love for Soraya Withstand Political Pressures* appeared. The speed with which the speculative articles appeared was remarkable.

As early as September 1951, just seven months after their wedding, the announcement of Soraya having a short holiday with her mother in Switzerland was sufficient for the international press to begin speculating about the marriage. Usually claiming to be facts from impeccable sources, headlines included *Soraya's Life in Danger*, *Soraya's Dream Journey*, or even *Soraya and The Mysterious Child* circulated. Some articles claimed she was mentally ill with an incurable disease.

At the height of the Mosaddeq riots, papers were claiming the

Shah and Soraya had fled to Rome so she could give birth to a child – a girl. The birth was kept secret as the child was not "normal" and was given to a convent.

In the summer of 1954, several gossip columns made out Soraya was expecting. During her pregnancy, so-called updates made out she was very ill and was under the care of a Swiss gynaecologist. Despite there being a plethora of photos of her at her girls' summer camps on the Caspian Sea!

The rumours of a pending divorce gave the journalists a free hand to write whatever they liked. Before 1957, the Iranian Royal Court did not have its own press office to make official releases. Foreign journalists who printed anything not approved by the Shah were sanctioned and banned from entering Iran. Once prohibited, the journalists had no inhibitions as there were no deterrents; made-up stories proliferated. The stories' prohibition in Iran guaranteed Soraya never had the opportunity to read the nonsense, but false news ran riot in the tabloids of Europe and America.

Separating articles of questionable accuracy from the truth is nigh impossible. A lengthy article appeared on 17th July 1957 in an Australian weekly that maintained Iranian couples without issue were regarded as being cursed. It alleged the Shah's mother and his twin sister were openly expressing their opinion that Soraya was so afflicted.

It went on to state that the Shah and Soraya had recently been yachting in the Mediterranean and sunbathing in Capri. From there, they had travelled to Switzerland where they saw several gynaecologists. Yet, during this period, all the Pahlavis were at Saadabad. The so-called exposé asserted Soraya was telling people she had had enough of being medically examined. The scoop revealed that a Russian gynaecologist was telling journalists that the problem was with the Shah; there was nothing wrong with Soraya. Further assertions included Soraya's typhoid had been caused by fanatical priests deliberately poisoning her as they were bitterly opposed to the marriage.

While recovering from the typhoid, the Shah unquestionably had pampered her every wish; to what extent, however, is open to conjecture. Supposedly, when she asked to listen to classical music, a radiogram appeared two hours later with one hundred records. When she said she would like some chocolate truffles, the Iranian ambassador in Switzerland was ordered to get a box of Sprungli's specials and have them flown at once to Tehran. The truth of her strict diet, being monitored by Dr Ayadi and Aunt Forough, would have sold fewer papers.

Claiming to be factual, an article in one journal described Soraya as spoiled because she grew up in luxury. Asserting Eva Karl was an heiress, it proclaimed Soraya's childhood was spent shuttling between Berlin and Isfahan. No mention was made of the reasons: the pressures on Khalil due to the anti-Bakhtiari stance by the Tehran Government and the Nazi's policy of conscription in 1936. The same journal asserted Soraya had a Teutonic, brusque manner. Not afraid to speak her mind, she would often get into trouble. It alleged that at an unidentified, public dinner party, she strongly disagreed with her husband, had a tantrum, picked up a vase, and threw it at a wall, smashing it to pieces. At another unknown dinner party, the Shah had joked to the guests that Soraya was his kind of woman. She purportedly retorted by saying she couldn't say the same about him. I questioned her behaviour with her cousin; I was assured Soraya always behaved impeccably in company.

Another tale, widely spread, was that if she couldn't get her own way, she would ban the Shah from entering her bedroom, sometimes for weeks. When approached by a servant to let the Shah return to their bedroom, she told him where he could stick it.

Such yarns aroused the readers' interest and increased sales, but are without basis. At one point, Mosaddeq was accused of declaring in parliament that the Shah must get rid of "the childless German woman". This is grossly untrue, as in both her biographies, Soraya asserts the relationship between them was one of a distant respect for each other.

Contentions that Soraya scorned royal customs, and avoided tedious royal duties, thereby being a bad queen, were vehemently denied by her cousins who both stressed how popular she was with the people. The masses who demonstrated their feelings for Soraya by gathering outside the Echtessassi Palace and shouting for her to remain when it became common knowledge that her divorce from the Shah was inevitable prove this.

Another rumour claimed Soraya was jealous of Princess Shahnaz. It asserted that Soraya was responsible for sending Shahnaz to a Swiss boarding school, thereby cutting her out of the Shah's life. Shahnaz was born in 1940 and had started boarding school before Soraya came on the scene.

The trip to America in 1954 was considered a success other than for the whisper that Soraya was infertile. An article in a US newspaper reported that the gynaecologists in New York had confirmed that there was nothing wrong, but that the Shah and Soraya then went to Boston, for a second opinion. There, a specialist gave the couple the heart-breaking diagnosis that the queen was barren and could never have a baby. It was pure fabrication, as after sightseeing in New York, they went directly to Washington to meet President Eisenhower. At no time were they in Boston.

The divorce announcement created a massive amount of publicity in the international press. However, details continued to differ for weeks. One account claimed that the Shah's statement on Tehran Radio on 21st March 1958 came as a total shock to Soraya. She was apparently astonished. The piece claimed Soraya had been expecting the Shah to announce he was giving up his crown, like King Edward VIII for Wallis Simpson. This allegation is false as we know the forlorn hope delegation had twice tried to find an eleventh-hour solution. The story can only have been an attempt to get the readers' sympathy on Soraya's side.

The details of the divorce settlement are full of made-up figures. Soraya's biographies asserted that she managed on her investments. The press disagreed; although the size of the Shah's monthly allowance was unclear.

Over the years, weekly and monthly magazines occasionally reported the Shah and Soraya still loved each other and met in secret. Several times in both her biographies Soraya emphasised she never saw him after leaving Tehran.

In 1979, when it became clear the Shah was dying of cancer, Soraya reputedly wrote him a letter. The letter, by all accounts, told the Shah that she still loved him and wished to see him. His reply supposedly confessed that he had never stopped loving her and was desperate to say goodbye. However, he pointed out that his wife, Farah, was with him and they would have to wait until he was recuperating alone in Cairo. Soraya makes no mention of such correspondence in her biographies.

Inexplicably, there are many errors in Krause's book and in Soraya's two autobiographies. All three books state Soraya was sixteen when she married. Krause tells the reader that Soraya was born on her parent's third wedding anniversary. Krause claimed Eva and Khalil returned to Isfahan in the autumn of 1939 – unimaginable as Hitler had invaded Poland on 1st September and traveling from Berlin to Iran via Moscow would have been impossible. This mistake would have meant Bijan being born in Germany. Another claim was that, after the Shah's 1948 divorce from Empress Fawzieh, he became engaged to the daughter of Hussein Ala, later his Prime Minister. The engagement is not mentioned in any other literature.

Krause asserts that Soraya never saw her grandparents after leaving Berlin in 1939 until 1955 when she was queen, but the family moved to Zurich in 1947 for Eva to look after her parents.

Soraya claims in both her biographies that she was named after the constellation Ursa Major, as her name means seven stars. Ursa Major does have seven stars. However, she was named after the constellation Plaidies, also with seven stars, as the name of her Imperial Order of the Plaidies proves.

21

AFTERMATH OF DIVORCE

A New Beginning

Khalil and Eva's residence was the official Iranian embassy in Cologne. Not wanting to live in a government house, Soraya rented a small house nearby. However, without her knowing, the Shah had granted her the title of "Imperial Princess", placing her on the same level as Shams and Ashraf. The designation included a diplomatic passport for life which meant all Iranian embassies worldwide were at her disposal. She remained a detached member of the royal family, whether she liked it or not.

She had hoped the paparazzi would stop chasing her, but the long-distance, telephoto lenses continued snapping away at their target. The cameras haunted her day and night. The tabloids began speculating she was suicidal as her sad face suggested she was missing her husband – anything for a scoop.

To escape from the unwanted publicity, in May, Eva and Soraya organized a holiday to America. Together with Bijan, they sailed to Bermuda via New York hoping for peace and sunshine. However, their plan didn't work. The party was spotted changing ships in New York. *Life Magazine* ran a feature soon after they arrived in Bermuda, including photos of Soraya playing tennis. After that, Bermuda was swamped with journalists.

Settled in a comfortable cottage overlooking Hamilton Harbour, Soraya took up the traditional pleasures of a tourist. She slept late most mornings before taking a leisurely breakfast. She then went water skiing – her favourite sport since acquiring the skill with the Shah on the Caspian Sea. Professional skiers commented favourably on her ability. She sunbathed on the sands and took afternoon tea at the local tennis club. Occasionally she went out in the evenings with her mother and brother. She always appeared preoccupied, unsurprising with hidden cameras never far away. On several fishing expeditions, with local fishermen, she clearly enjoyed making a catch. The three enjoyed themselves sufficiently to stay an extra week beyond their planned fortnight.

The Divorce Settlement

Much controversy surrounded the divorce settlement, as no details were made public. In both Soraya's biographies, she went to extraordinary lengths to claim that the sums of money were considerably smaller than was commonly publicised. She admits she kept her personal property including her jewels, retained her wedding dress and a few souvenirs that had been given in the course of her travels.

She did acknowledge, however, that the Shah gave her several farms with large areas of land as security. She did not elaborate, other than to explain that under Iranian Law widows were entitled to no more than 8% of their husband's estate. Assuming this is true, then the communes could only have been given to ensure she received more than the 8% figure. She admitted that her capital was invested to give her sufficient funds to live in comfort. The problem was that much of her wealth was invested in Iran, necessitating her father to return to Tehran from time to time, to deal with any problems. In both her biographies, she passionately denied receiving a monthly allowance for life from the Shah. She insisted that after the divorce, she lived entirely on her own income and was not dependent on him.

To quote from her father's favourite Shakesperian play, *the lady doth protest too much, methinks*. Estimates of the Shah's personal wealth varied. A conservative figure of US $500 million in 1959, widely published in US papers, was believed to be accurate. The figure reflects the Consortium Agreement of 1954 with BP, since when the Shah had been receiving 5% of the oil profits tax free.

Despite Soraya's claims of a prudent, penny-wise existance, her post-divorce, jet-setting lifestyle can only be described as hyper-luxurious by the standards of the time. She described spending the summer of 1960 in Greece, Portofino and Monte Carlo before flying to Los Angeles – an expensive way of living by any standards.

Several sources claimed Soraya received a lump sum of US $67,000 plus a monthly allowance of US $7,000. Today that would be worth at least thirty to fifty times that amount. She was given two cars: a Rolls-Royce and a Mercedes sports car. The Shah reputedly gave her an undisclosed sum of jewels valued at over tens of thousands of dollars. Her engagement ring, a 22.37 carat solitaire, was eventually sold for US $800,000 after her death. Undisputed is that the Shah bought her a small estate in Marbella; the hideaway became her refuge from the paparazzi.

Articles in *The New York Times* and *The Washington Post*, published after the Shah's death in 1980, claimed his fortune was well above US $2 billion. His father's vast amounts of land, acquired during his reign, were used by the Shah to obtain shares in all the major enterprises in Iran. The Pahlavis, thereby, had built up huge holdings in the nation's banks, factories and businesses.

After their divorce, the Shah formed the Pahlavi Foundation and transferred his holdings to a charitable family trust. Coupled with receiving 5% of Iran's share of the oil profits, the Pahlavi wealth was only rivalled by that of the royal family of Saudi Arabia. In the last three years of his reign, the Pahlavi Foundation transferred up to US $4 billion from Iran to the United States according to *The New York Times*. Soraya's cousin assured me that additional resources were deposited in Swiss banks and off-shore accounts world-wide.

Queen Farah Diba

Less than eighteen months after Soraya's divorce, in the autumn of 1959, the Shah surprisingly announced his engagement to a twenty-one year old Iranian, Farah Diba. The Shah had met her in Paris in 1958 when she was one of several Iranian students on scholarships at the Sorbonne. At the time, Farah was engaged to a fellow Iranian student. However, after meeting the Shah, a scheming Farah saw her chance to become Empress of Iran. But to placate her fiancé, in her memoir *An Enduring Love: My Life with the Shah*, published in 2005, Farah controversially admitted she promised her ex-fiancé and true love that he would *always be by her side*. She appointed him to be "Secretary to the Office of the Empress" for life. The rumour in the Court was that he remained her lover while the Shah was being entertained elsewhere by Madame Claude's working girls. Even ardent supporters of the Pahlavi regime in the Court, including General Yazdan-Panah, were privately discussing the obvious "what if" scenario: could the couple's future son and, therefore, heir to the throne be less eligible than the Shah's half-brother. Royalists in the Majlis were having doubts about the monarchy's long-term future.

The Shah and Farah married on 22nd December 1959. By October 1960, a son, Reza, and heir presumptive to the throne, was born. In Soraya's first biography, published in 1963, Soraya unconvincingly wrote she wished them well, a feeling not generally felt in the Court.

In the same chapter, Soraya's sad reflection of her role in the saga of the Iranian Royal Family was balanced by a determined resolution to begin a new life.

It was not until October 1967 that the Shah decided to crown Farah as Queen. By then, another child, a girl, had been born. The couple remained together until the Shah's death; by then, two further children had been born – a boy and a girl.

Around this time, Iran's oil revenues were growing rapidly to the point that America's influence was weakening. The US support for the Mosaddeq coup now counted for little in the Shah's eyes; he believed he was invincible. Consequently, American, and European, media began a critical campaign that influenced younger Iranians, particularly those students being educated in the West where liberal ideas were sowing the seeds for social change.

Soraya makes no mention of the coronation in her second autobiography, published in 1990. However, she must have noticed that Farah's crown was not the one designed for her coronation. The new crown was made for Farah by Van Cleef and Arpels of Paris with jewels belonging to the Shah, whose wealth meant he no longer needed to borrow them from the Iranian Government.

It is interesting to read in Farah's memoir, *An Enduring Love: My Life with the Shah*, that she described having similar problems to those of Soraya with Nimtaj and Princess Ashraf.

The Nobel 200

In 1961, Soraya realised she needed an occupation. She had met a German-born industrialist, who had immigrated to Britain before WWII. Ten years older than Soraya, his adopted name was York Nobel. The Managing Director of York Nobel Industries had served in the British Army for the final two years of the war on intelligence duties. His company had begun to produce a bubble car, the Nobel 200 in 1957, based on the German Messerschmitt and Heinkel bubble cars. Built by Short Brothers and Harland in Northern Ireland, its three-wheel, glass-fibre body had a German Sachs engine.

York Nobel knew the car's profile needed to be raised if it was to sell in any quantity. He appointed Mike Hawthorn, the 1958 Formula One World Champion, to become the company's Technical Director amidst great publicity at the Paris Motor Show. Sadly, Hawthorn was to die in a car accident on the Guildford Bypass in Surrey in January 1959. With a similar idea for the promoting the car's advertising, Soraya was offered the position of public relations director. She accepted, but never took-up the position as the company ceased production in 1961 as a result of strikes at the shipbuilding yards in Belfast that affected the whole of engineering manufacturing in Northern Ireland.

Shah's Popularity Plummets Further

In May 1961, 50,000 school teachers went on strike. The Shah thought it may have been organised by the CIA. A year later, when university students and staff joined the protests, he sacked his prime Minister, Ali Amani. The Shah replaced Amani with his closest ally, Asadollah Alam, a tyrant who effectively took control of running the country. On his orders, SAVAK shot dozens of students at a demonstration in Tehran. Panicking, the Shah sacked its leader, Teymour Bakhtiar, and expelled him from Iran. He had, perhaps without realizing the consequences, dismissed the two most influential players in overthrowing Mosaddeq: Zahedi and Teymour.

After visiting President Kennedy at the White House in April 1962, the Shah returned to proclaim women were to be given the vote, thinking the liberal move would be seen as being democratic and restore his flagging popularity. Unknowingly, he had put another nail in his coffin. The senior Iman, Ayatollah Khomeini, argued that the fate of Iran must not be decided by women. Supportive protests sprung-up all over Iran. In the holy city of Qom, 200 protestors were killed. The Shah had no option but to exile Khomeini to Iraq. No fool, Khomeini, on learning Saddam Hussein was planning to assassinate him, fled to France.

22

MALE FRIENDSHIPS

After her divorce, admirers soon began gathering around Soraya. She confessed the male attention left her confused. She had not experienced the hurly-burly of teenage life, apart from minor mischief at boarding school against the code of conduct which was designed to restrict contact with the opposite sex. Aged eighteen and with no experience of social mixing with boys, she had married the Shah, the first man with whom she had physical contact.

Divorced and aged twenty-six, she was totally innocent about masculine manoeuvres or their intentions. She found it difficult to differentiate between men she could trust or those seeking publicity when accompanying her. When seen with male escorts, the photographs of Soraya with her latest beau made headline news in the glossy journals. In Iran, such magazines were forbidden. The Shah's government was attempting to whitewash Soraya out of the people's memory.

Prince Johannes von Thurn

Soraya met the openly bisexual 11th Prince Johannes von Thurn und Taxis, six years older than her, on 31st December 1958 at a party in

St. Moritz. He was the richest man in West Germany. His father, the 10th Prince, had left his entire fortune to his future, unborn great-grandson, the 13th Prince. The tax fiddle to avoid death duties, estimated to be worth US $500 million, was the biggest tax fraud up to that time. Therefore, Johannes's inheritance was strictly not his. However, having inherited the management of the family's 700 estates in Germany, he had his hand on the till. In order to keep the wealth in the family, in May 1980, he married Countess Gloria von Schönburg, thirty-four years younger. Their third child was a boy – the 12th Prince von Thurn und Taxis.

Von Thurn was to remain a close friend and confidant to Soraya for all her life. When she wanted a platonic friendship after her divorce, he had comforted her. She frequently recommended him to friends if they wanted investment advice. Over the years, he considerably increased her assets by protecting her from unscrupulous financial advisers.

Maximilian Schell

In the early 1960s, Maximilian Schell had a two-year affair with Soraya, during which time he won the 1961 Oscar for Best Actor in the film, *Judgment at Nuremberg*. Schell shared German roots with Soraya. During their friendship they would tease each other when they noticed the paparazzi photographing them. They would have a small bet with each other on which magazine's front cover they would appear.

Soraya was frequently seen with him on location during his film shoots. He introduced her, on one occasion, to the actress Ursula Andress, who was about to play the lead role in the film *She*. For fun, Ursula proposed Soraya could take a cameo role where she would be a belly-dancer. Soraya agreed providing her name was not listed in the cast. Perhaps embarrassed by her performance, Soraya makes no mention of her escapade in either of her biographies. The film was released without Soraya's scene. The film is not generally considered a success.

Soon after their breakup in the spring of 1962, Schell was rumored to have become engaged to the first Afro-American supermodel, Dony Luna. In 1986, he married the Russian actress Natalya Andrejchenko. They had a daughter, Nastassja, born in 1989. After divorcing, Schell married a German opera singer, Iva Mihanovic, in 2013.

In 1930, Schell had been born into a Roman Catholic family in Vienna. However, in 1938 the family fled the Anschluss and moved to Basel, Switzerland, where Maximilian went to school and university. He served in the Swiss army and then, aged twenty-two, embarked on a professional acting career. Handsome, he had a strong screen presence and was articulate in both German and English. By the late-fifties he was playing in films with Marlon Brando and on stage with Rosemary Harris in New York. After playing Hamlet on Broadway, he portrayed the defence layer in *Judgement at Nuremberg*, where, despite first-rate performances by Spencer Tracy and Burt Lancaster, Schell won the Oscar for the best actor. He died aged 83 in 2014.

Gunter Sachs

Gunter Sachs was born in southern Germany in November 1932. A grandson of the car manufacturer Wilhelm von Opel, Sachs's wealth helped him to become a prominent member of the glamorous 1960s jet-set. He was a playboy photographer who gained fame as a documentary film-maker. He had an affair with Soraya from mid-1962 to early 63. A gifted sportsman, he had met Soraya on the ski slopes in St Moritz.

Later in 1966, after meeting Brigitte Bardot in the south of France, Sachs arranged for a helicopter to fly over her house in St Tropez and drop hundreds of red roses. 'It's not every day that a man drops a ton of roses in your yard,' Bardot famously wrote. Soon after, he married her in Las Vegas. The marriage lasted just over three years.

He was granted Swiss nationality when he became Chairman of the St Moritz Bobsleigh Club in 1969. Sachs was further married three times. He often boasted of never having worked a day in his life. He died when he shot himself in 2011, leaving an estimated US $1.5 billion.

Prince Raimondo Orsini

The only suitor mentioned by name in Soraya's two autobiographies is Prince Raimondo Orsini. Their friendship attracted the attention of the paparazzi soon after her split from Sachs.

Courtesy Alamy Images
With Prince Raimondo Orsini

Their romance was notorious as Orsini's lineage was far stronger than the Pahlavi family. The Orsini family could boast five popes, including Nicholas III, 1277–1280, and Benedict XIII, 1724–1730, as well as thirty cardinals. The family's history gave Raimondo the right to the title of Assistant Prince to the Papal Throne. Consequently, he could attend papal ceremonies sitting on the right-hand side of the Pope – the highest hereditary lay position in the Vatican.

Countless journalists followed them as their friendship flourished. A rumour spread that Soraya was converting to Roman Catholicism as they planned to wed.

However, Orsini began to receive threatening letters. Written in a primitive script and signed with a Muslim name, one letter warned that if he continued to see Soraya then he would be shot. Orsini didn't take the threats seriously, but Soraya persuaded him that the police must get involved.

Nevertheless, the inconvenience of being guarded day and night didn't prevent them going to Capri together in the summer of 1963. Soraya was twelve years older and wiser than when she had met the Shah, and it proved sufficient for her to question making a marital commitment. Their friendship fizzled out. The gossip weeklies speculated, incorrectly according to Soraya, that the Shah had forbidden her to remarry on pain of losing her allowances.

Orsini's wealth allowed him to live an extremely comfortable life. He was fifty when he married a Georgian princess and subsequently had four children. He died in 2020, aged eighty-nine.

Hugh O'Brian

A chapter in Soraya's first autobiography is titled *My admirers and I*. She referred to several of her unnamed suitors as good friends but denied she had a serious relationship with anyone. She insisted all the reports about her alleged marriage plans were premature.

However, a chance visit to America provided her with a respite. In October 1960, she flew to Los Angeles and stayed with friends. There she met the TV actor Hugh O'Brian. Without naming him in her book, she describes him as the ideal hero-figure: silent, tough and clean-cut. She admitted feeling protected when he was about. She enjoyed entering a public place with him as all eyes turned on him; it was a blessing for the attention to be on someone else. Hugh O'Brian followed her to Europe to sell his TV rights in Britain. The press concluded there a marriage was in the air. Again, this proved false. Most famous for playing Wyatt Earp in the TV series, *The Life and Legend of Wyatt Earp*, he appeared in western movies such as *The Man from the Alamo, The Shootist* and *Broken Lance*.

Other Affairs

Being chased by paparazzi, Soraya's life was subjected to countless rumours of unproven romances. She was said to have ignored the seductive advances of Hollywood's Kirk Douglas, but conversely to have spent a night with Frank Sinatra, as well as succumbing to the charms of Mel Ferrer. Even the gay actor Rock Hudson was not indifferent to her charms. True or false, one thing was certain: Soraya's enigmatic beauty left no one indifferent.

Countless Interviews

Countless glossy magazines sought to interview her. The fees she charged were not disclosed, but she happily modelled for their professional photographers to ensure the front cover would make a splash.

In her interviews, she was happy to give details of her early life, such as when living with her parents in Germany. She admitted that, after her divorce, she kept bumping into people in the crowded streets. She had grown accustomed to everyone moving to one side when in her presence. She had no idea how to order a meal in a restaurant because she had never had to make a choice. She thought the waiter should be tipped before the meal to ensure special attention. This habit actually became her usual custom.

The most humorous reply to questions occurred in one interview, when asked what was the most useful thing she received in her divorce settlement. She replied, 'My diplomatic passport'. The follow-up question enquired why. Without hesitation, her answer, was it allowed her to park her car wherever she wished!

23

THE THREE FACES OF A WOMAN

Dino de Laurentis

In January 1964, Soraya met Dino de Laurentis at a private party in Beverley Hills. She had met him on several previous occasions, but that evening he continued to press her to consider a career as a movie actress. De Laurentis was one of the producers who had brought Italian cinema to the international scene after WWII. He eventually produced some 500 films, of which thirty-eight were nominated for Oscars.

It had been five years since Soraya left Tehran. Living the life of a lady of leisure had become boring. As a girl, she had dreamt of becoming a film actress. Consequently, she showed interest, asking questions about what it would entail. That evening, they agreed she should take a screen test.

In March, they met in Rome. For a fortnight she read scripts and dissected them with de Laurentis and possible directors, who were mostly unknown to her. Soraya had insisted news of the tests must not leak out, so they were secretly held at a private studio. The technicians and make-up artists had to agree to a confidentiality clause in their contracts. The tests began in the late evening, took four hours, and didn't finish until the early hours of the following morning. Taking all the black and white, colour, close-ups, and longer shots left her exhausted.

The following day, de Laurentis declared the screen tests were a success and a contract was signed.

The film, to be called *The Three Faces of a Woman*, would be shot at the end of the year. It consisted of three, linked, short stories. Each was to be directed by three dissimilar directors who Soraya could choose. Soraya insisted on certain clauses in the contract. Firstly, the credits only showed her first name, Soraya. Secondly, if she felt scenes were not appropriate, she would not be obliged to do them. Possibly afraid of either the Shah's or her father's reaction, this clause included kissing and embracing. Sometime after the film was made, she denied this limitation in a BBC TV interview. The restrictions almost stopped the film being made, as one of the directors, Antonioni, insisted that Soraya's partner should take her in his arms and kiss her.

De Laurentis eventually agreed that the kiss would not be on the lips, but a peck on the cheeks, and the embrace would be "demure".

Franco Indovina

De Laurentis proposed three directors for the film, to be titled *Il Tre Volti*. Soraya accepted the first two directors, Michelangelo Antonioni and Mauro Bolognini. However, she objected to the third, Franco Indovina, on the grounds that he was unknown. She thought he would jeopardize the quality of the film.

There was an impasse. De Laurentis explained that Antonioni would quit if Indovina was not chosen. Finally, she agreed to meet him. He arrived with de Laurentis. After introductions, he began to show Soraya sketches of his ideas. Soraya was instantly caught in his spell and hardly listened. As his hands excitedly expressed his enthusiasm, and his fingers flashed across his drawings, his eyes were full of sparkle. Soraya was hooked. At the age of 32, Soraya was truly in love for the first time.

The Three Faces

The scenes of the first story, *Il Provino*, were shot in Venice and Athens with Bolognini directing. Soraya found the routine – up at dawn, make-up, the heat of the lights, the whirl of cameras, the special effects, tracking shots, reverse shots, quick snack-meals, and preparation for the following day – invigorating. She never tired. She was in her element, doing what she had always wanted to do as a teenager.

The second story, *Gli Amanti Celebri*, was shot in Rome, much of it in a studio. Antonioni directed what seemed countless scenes. Indovina attended, making suggestions when asked. In the story, Soraya's opposite number was the Irish actor, Richard Harris. Harris was reported as saying that the Princess had the same star quality and talent as Grace Kelly. After work, the evenings were a continuous round of dinner parties in local restaurants or at the homes of the cast. An unusual feature of the film was that three languages were used: English, French, and Italian. The actors skipped from one to another in an apparently random fashion. Although not fluent in Italian, Soraya mechanically learnt her words. Critics would later criticise her Italian as having a strong German accent.

The third story, directed by Indovina, was called *Latin Lover*. Soraya's friendship with Indovina blossomed despite him hardly being able to speak a word of French and she little Italian. They exchanged conspiratorial glances as they plotted the best way to satisfy their mutual feelings. He brushed against her whenever he could; she

Courtesy Alamy Images

With Richard Harris her opposite partner in *Gli Amanti Celebri*.

responded despite her natural reserve. Her aloofness as an empress was breaking down.

She was feeling a blinding passion for the first time. Secretly, Soraya took lessons in Italian to better understand his feelings while, unknown to her, he started learning French. Within six weeks, she had learnt sufficient Italian to hold a meaningful conversation. She discovered the intensity of her feelings was reciprocated. When they spoke, whether on the set or at the evening parties, everything they talked about was important. They discovered they shared interests in painting, literature and politics.

The flowering of their passion was not possible, however, for

Indovina was married with two children. Once Soraya learnt this, she realised her love had to be sacrificed before it could begin. It was torture on set; working with him made her unhappy. As a consequence, her acting suffered after what had been a promising start.

According to Soraya's cousin, Soraya's participation in making the film had been kept quiet from the Shah. However, leaks had occurred and it soon became the main topic discussed behind the back of the Pahlavis in Court. Everyone in Court was anticipating seeing it. The film was released at the Milan Film Festival in February 1965. The critics hammered it. Soraya's acting was described as uninspiring, wooden, lifeless, and dull. The film was a total flop.

Twenty-one copies of the film were printed, only one remains – in the Italian Film Archives in Rome. The others mysteriously disappeared. Soraya believed the Shah had paid a fortune to de Laurentis to have them destroyed. In her second biography, Soraya's bitterness is made abundantly clear. Her words refer to it being typical of the Shah "to remove the image of the very woman who had shattered his image". The acrimonious comment in her 1992 book was made thirty-four years after her divorce. That her resentment had lasted so long cannot go unnoticed. She was, at last, accepting that her teenage, schoolgirl crush on her king had been a terrible mistake.

The widespread belief that the Shah had the copies destroyed was generally accepted within the Royal Court. The bitterness among the courtiers was similar to that of their former empress. They realised the Shah was still envious of Soraya's success and popularity with his subjects.

Soraya left Rome and returned to her rented apartment in Munich. For two years, she had brief friendships while all the time thinking only of her beloved Franco. It took the suicide of a close friend from her schooldays to shake her out of her depression. She realised she had squandered her life. She was thirty-three and had come to a crossroads. It was time to turn the corner and meet Franco again.

A Teenager at Last

In 1966, Soraya returned to Rome, rented a suite of rooms in a premier hotel and sent invitations to about ten friends, including Indovina, for an evening party. He accepted. As she waited for him to arrive, her heart pounded, her legs trembled, and she took a whisky to calm her nerves. The others in the drawing-room, nibbling their canapés and drinking champagne, didn't know why she was so nervous.

When the doorbell rang, she rushed to open it ahead of the waiter. He stood tall and slim, a smile on his face. They hugged – a breathtakingly short embrace before introducing him to everyone. There followed the usual polite trivia that seemed to drag on and on, as they wanted to be alone. When one of the party suggested they leave for a restaurant, they all agreed to meet at a local bistro.

Soraya and Franco were the last to leave in his car. He started up the engine and drove away in the opposite direction, suggesting they spent the night alone. They drove around, finding a quiet spot under the pine trees at the Villa Medici.

They held each other and talked about the intervening two years that had been wasted. They kissed and agreed their future together was all that mattered. They returned to her hotel and spent the night together in her suite as they lost themselves with each other.

The following afternoon, she flew back to Munich. He left for the Cinecittà Studios where he was making a film. Having separated from his wife, Indovina and Soraya began spending every weekend together, usually managing to escape the paparazzi. Soraya admitted a back alley frequently provided a location for a secret kiss as they revelled in the intense excitement of not being seen. She felt young again. An immense load had been lifted from her shoulders. Within a couple of weeks, Soraya rented a villa in Rome with a large garden filled with flowers, trees and a swimming pool. Franco moved in.

It gave them a degree of privacy that allowed them to lie in bed looking at the stars. The villa became a part of them.

Franco's contrast with the Shah was as different as chalk to cheese. The Shah was an introvert. Indovina was a bohemian, socially unconventional. It was this characteristic that Soraya found attractive as it reflected her younger self. She loved the simplicity of not having to disguise her feelings. She could say what she wanted. She had become young and as carefree as her days as a student in Switzerland.

24

SIX HAPPY YEARS

Life with Franco

For Soraya, living with Indovina was like living at home with her parents as a youngster. Their house was full of laughter, freedom to talk honestly, and, above all, the absence of the bitter, petty rivalries and jealousies that had dominated the Pahlavi family.

Life was unpretentious: a lazy, late breakfast, with no pre-planned programme on which to be briefed. They would stretch out on the rugs and talk intellectually on the great matters affecting the world such as why the Americans were in Vietnam, the six-day war in Israel, or the assassination of Che Guevara. They discovered they both liked the same literature, and Swedish films, such as Ingmar Bergman's *The Seventh Seal*. Franco taught her how to cook pasta *al dente*.

On Sundays, they invited Franco's friends to their home. Many did not know Soraya and treated her informally. She soon became a member of their band of kindred spirits. She became friendly with Antonioni, director of the second story of *The Three Faces*. Soraya had always felt that Antonioni had seen her as a smug dilettante, superficially acting to become an instant filmstar. She wondered if de Laurentis may have conned Antonioni into accepting the commission;

she was left with the impression that he resented and regretted undertaking it. However, after several visits to their home, and seeing Soraya bore no resentment for the film's failure, he expressed his satisfaction with her performance in *Gli Amanti Celebri*. Others to become friends included Federico Fellini, Franco Zefirelli, Carlo Ponti, Monica Vitti, and Peter O'Toole.

While some would insist on cooking gargantuan amounts of pasta with *fruits de mer*, others would play cards, talk about their latest book, or recount an exhibition they had recently visited. Subjects on the agenda included art, films, and politics.

During the week, the couple would shut their doors. Lazing on a rug in their lounge, while examining sketches for Franco's next film, was total bliss. However, the paparazzi continued to plague their lives whenever they could. To find freedom and fresh inspiration, over their years together, Indovina and Soraya escaped to places such as Morocco, Tunisia, and the Caribbean.

Soon after moving back to Rome, Soraya had found herself receiving invitations to balls from Italian high society. Having previously found the lifestyle artificial, she wanted no more. With Franco refusing to go with her, she declined the invitations. Franco never asked her about her life in Tehran, realising she had had an unhappy time. He had the knack of making her laugh, thereby keeping her happy. She had found total contentment at last.

May 1972 – Disaster

General elections were held in Italy on 7th May 1972 to select the Sixth Republic Parliament. Franco had retained his name on the electoral list of his former home town, Palermo, in Sicily. Keen to vote, he asked Soraya to accompany him for a brief holiday, promising they could go fishing – a pastime she enjoyed.

Soraya made excuses. She did not wish to meet Franco's wife and daughters. Eva's birthday was 11th May. It was a reason to go to Munich where her parents had retired. Franco promised to be away for no more than ten days. On 5th May, Franco took an evening flight from Rome to Palermo, a distance of approximately 260 miles – a flight time of under two hours. The flight took-off thirty-six minutes late with 108 passengers and a crew of seven. Both pilots were highly experienced. The flight contacted Palermo approach around 9:30pm stating it was seventy-four miles from touchdown. Half an hour later, in darkness, it crashed into Mount Longa, 1,980 feet, southwest of Palermo. The aircraft had struck the mountain a few metres below its summit and disintegrated on impact. All 115 occupants were killed. At the time of the accident, the visibility was limited to two miles with clouds down to 1,500 feet. The wreckage was strewn across the mountain. It took three hours for rescue teams to reach the site.

Later, some witnesses at the nearby village of Carini said that they had seen the aircraft on fire before the crash. The 108 passengers were, for the most part, returning home to vote in the Italian national elections.

The official inquiry blamed the pilots for not following the orders of the air traffic controllers. The reason for the crash was recorded as pilot error. However, there was another widely held belief. Some of the victims' relatives, many years later, found a report written by the local vice-chief of police that stated the plane had exploded because of a bomb. The report accused the Mafia and a subversive right-wing group with responsibility. The National Association of Italian Pilots defended the aircrew, refusing to believe pilot error was the cause owing to their long experience.

Who Were "They"?

On the day previous to Franco's flight, Soraya had left for Munich. Eva was upset that Soraya had been unable to bring Franco. Eva adored him, knowing how happy he had made her daughter. Khalil had always showed restraint when hearing of Soraya's menfolk. Although soon to be forty years of age, Soraya still found it difficult to discuss her male relationships with her father.

On the evening of the 5th May, Soraya went to bed feeling lonely. She tossed and turned until 2.00am when she got up to have a drink. When she finally fell asleep, she claimed she had nightmares. She awoke to the incessant ringing of the telephone. Looking at her watch, it was only 4.00am. She went downstairs to pick up the receiver. It was Franco's cousin. He gave her the news that Franco's plane had crashed, but search parties were looking through the debris for survivors and she mustn't give up hope.

She was numb. It was bad enough that people thought she was barren, but now she had been robbed of Franco – the knight in shining armour who had given her faith, hope and love. She felt fated to a life of false dawns; the last six years had been a dream. All she could think of was holding hands, his smile, his voice, their nights of madness, and their non-stop happiness.

See bibliography – Francesco Terracina
Franco and Soraya, 1972

Her mother understood her desolation, but knew remaining silent was best to allow Soraya recover.

Franco was buried in Palermo. His wife and daughters were present. Soraya was not. She felt bitter – her life had been nothing but a mess. In her biography, she wrote that, "They had killed Franco".

Whether she suspected the Shah had a hand in the possible bombing, or not, is uncertain. There is no evidence, only hints by conspiracy theorists. In 1972, however, the Shah's secret police, the SAVAK, was ruthlessly controlling life in Iran. It had been established by the Shah with the help of the CIA. SAVAK operated from 1956 until the Iranian Revolution of 1979, when it was dissolved. SAVAK's practice of torturing and executing opponents of the Pahlavi regime during those years was widespread. Highly unpopular among, not only the people, but also the Court and upper classes, at its peak the organization had as many as 60,000 undercover agents.

It seems improbable that if the Shah had not wanted his former wife to have a permanent relationship with Indovina, he would have ordered Franco's assassination much sooner. The mysterious destruction of the twenty copies of *The Three Faces*, followed by the mystery of Soraya's partner's death, does raise the possibility of the Shah's wish to control Soraya's life. It was a belief widely accepted among the populace that the Shah had become a ruthless, loathsome despot.

Aftershock

After four days of remaining in her room, refusing to eat and wishing to be left alone for the rest of her life, her father knocked on the door and entered. He no longer had any misgivings about his daughter's love for Franco and they hugged each other while the tears poured down her face. After what seemed a long time, Khalil whispered two lines written by the 14th century Persian poet Hafiz:

What ill fortune it would be if a bird such as you
Were to lose its way in the country of sorrow.

She stopped crying and looked at her dad. A smile broke on her face. She had lost her lover but gained her father.

She returned to Rome to see their house. She caressed his favourite chair, blew the dust off his typewriter, stared at the dead leaves strewn on the swimming pool, opened the shutters, gazed at the path expecting Franco to appear, but felt only the cold silence. She had to get away to somewhere austere, and unemotional. She wanted a place where she would be unknown. She fled to Norway, with her loyal secretary, Fräulein Marie-Louise Sägemühl, who had been at her side through thick and thin. They took the coastal ship to the North Cape, both of them quietly marvelling at the stark beauty of the fjords. They stayed at Kirkenes where the daylight was perpetual, the silence deafening, and the isolation infinite, before returning to Bergen.

Soraya made an attempt to settle back in Rome, but the pain had not healed despite Franco's friends greeting her and talking as if he was still alive. Slowly, her life began to veer away from the group. She would attend parties, but talk too much. She would go out to dinner, but not taste the food. She would dance with partners, but hear neither the music nor their conversation. For almost two years, she killed time drifting in a sea of memories. When Franco's sister mentioned she was about to visit Palermo, Soraya asked her to place a bouquet of marguerites, Franco's favourite flowers, on his grave. It brought her to her senses. She needed to find a refuge. She chose Paris.

In early 1974, she found a flat on the Avenue Montaigne, near the Champs-Élysées. She contacted Dr Ayadi through her father. Ayadi persuaded the Shah to buy her the apartment she had chosen. When she died, it was sold for over $3 million.

She never returned to Rome, but the Shah's instant generosity suggested he had never stopped loving Soraya.

Paris

Paris became Soraya's home. Low in spirits, she shut herself off, becoming something of a recluse trying to forget Franco. She slowly built up her strength, gradually realising there had to be a future, but only if she showed her face. She began to be seen at the local hairdressers and in the bar of the Hotel Plaza Athénée opposite her apartment. She was forty-two and began making plans to explore her unknown world – the Far East and South America. The schoolgirl wanderlust had returned. One of her French friends, Edmée de la Rochefoucauld, encouraged her to meet younger people. At house parties there were socialites, wealthy students, fashion models and actors who never knew her background. Frequently, she was the oldest present and would find herself sitting alone in a corner. Having been starved of the excitement of falling in and out of love as a teenager and in her early twenties, it was inevitable that the natural urge to spread her wings would result in scandalous *affaires du cœur*.

Audouin de Barbot

Her most scandalous affair was with a Spanish minor prince, Audouin de Barbot, who was twenty years younger. In 1975, Soraya went to her favourite Greek island, Mykonos, for a holiday with the handsome Spaniard.

They managed to keep their holiday secret until a picture of them was taken as they were preparing to return to France.

The Spanish playboy had become her latest beau. Caught by the paparazzi, Soraya announced she was particularly happy to visit Greece after its recent restoration of democracy. She added diplomatically that Greece had the most handsome prime minister in the world. The Greek Premier, Constantine Karamanlis, regularly spent his holidays on Mykonos, enjoying its simple, quiet atmosphere.

In the Italian gossip journal *Gente* of 22nd November 1976, an article portrayed Soraya on its front cover with the headline: *Mysterious tragedy in Paris – Soraya's latest friend killed himself at the age of 25.* The article speculated that Audouin had committed suicide as a result of the breakup of their affair. No mention is made of their relationship in Soraya's biographies.

The shock of being remotely associated with Audouin's suicide must have hurt. She realised she had to turn her life around. She began to work hard to raise money for charities: the International Red Cross, Save the Children, and the Triple-A charity for animals in Marbella, near her summer villa. She renewed friendships with old school friends, and made new ones. However, the night life had taken its toll; inevitably her health suffered. Her beautiful, featured face began to show its age, although her green eyes never lost their sparkle. She put on weight and with it her elegance suffered.

She wandered through Europe buying unnecessary antique furniture and haute couture. She half-heartedly attended social functions where it was obvious to all that she was suffering badly from depression. In 1995, she began to have computer lessons at the first internet café in Paris, Cybercafé de Paris, situated across the road from her apartment. By coincidence, the owner, Ben Solms, had met Soraya at Edmée de la Rochefoucault's birthday party and both had spoken to each other in German.

It was the time when the internet began taking off. Solms suggested Soraya should take lessons. To his surprise, she agreed. She began learning the intricacies of using Google; she started searching for people or places she had known. She fascinated Solms with stories of people she had met; people that he had only read about. Together at the computer terminal, she admitted she had not been prepared for a normal life. On one occasion, she confessed that after her divorce she hadn't known how to make tea, as such matters were below the dignity of an empress. However, Solms noted that she always wore her 22-carat engagement ring, even though the Shah had been dead for over fifteen years.

25

THE SHAH'S DOWNFALL

Explanations for the Shah's eventual downfall in 1979 are many and varied. No single event can be solely attributed to Mohammed Reza Pahlavi's fall from grace. Unquestionably, it began with his divorce from Soraya in 1958. Publically accusing his wife of being responsible for their break-up went too far. The people saw Soraya had instigated everything possible to improve living standards – changes that none of the Pahlavis had done in their thirty years of incumbency. Letting it be known that he had offered to take a sigheh compounded the bitterness of his subjects. Having lost his queen, then, as in chess, he was on a downhill slide to checkmate.

After Zahedi's overthrow of Mosaddeq in August 1953, the royal couple's return from Rome had met a rapturous reception. The years following, including their return from the USSR in June 1956, had raised Iran's international status. Soraya's popularity, as a result of their world tours, had seen her reputation reach its climax. They knew the major reason was solely owing to Soraya's relentless determination to overcome her husband's apathy. Her success eradicating corruption had not gone unnoticed and had led to big improvements in health care for the poorer classes. Similarly, educational and housing standards saw immeasurable advances.

After the divorce, the Shah compounded his unpopularity. He approved various changes in government that had disastrous, unforeseen consequences. The Shah decided to improve state security. He allowed the CIA to advise him on setting-up a secret service – the SAVAK. Leaving the management to General Teymour Bakhtiar, it slowly grew evermore brutal, regularly putting in jail suspected opponents of the Shah without trial. The Shah thereby acquired unrivalled power over his citizens, the Majlis and the Army. His rule became evermore tyrannical and hated by the public.

SAVAK allowed the Shah to enforce censorship on TV, radio, and the press. Books had to have their text approved before printing. Encouraged by both his immediate family and "psychological pillars", discontent was growing from his people from whom he was largely isolated.

After the people's disapproval of his divorce, the Shah's headlong rush to marry Farah Diba was received by both the Court and the masses with indifference. Even the arrival of their first son was not greeted with enthusiasm. It was becoming public knowledge that Farah Diba was spending unlimited sums of money. The biggest, single event that did irreparable damage to the Shah's reputation was the celebration of the 2,500th anniversary of the First Persian Empire of King Cyrus, founded in 550BC. Strictly, the anniversary should, therefore, have been held in 1950AD. However, it was Farah who insisted the event should be held. The Shah was unsure of the celebration, but took advice about its scale. The lengthy consultations delayed the celebration as different plans were analysed with his most trusted advisers. His closest adviser was General Yazdan-Panah who, along with other advisers, advised him not to celebrate the anniversary in an ostentatious manner.

Queen Farah, with delusions of grandeur, wanted a pretentious celebration that had never been equalled by any other country. The Shah gave in to his wife's wish to spend $100 million on what amounted to a party at the ruins of Persepolis, King Cyrus' capital. A tented village was created covering an area of 160 acres – equivalent to about eighty football pitches. Sixty-two tents were decorated by Maison Jansen, the Paris-based interior design company.

In three large marquees, French chefs from Maxim's of Paris prepared the sumptuous meals served on Limoges porcelain with wine in Baccarat crystal glasses. One amusing incident occurred when the chefs from Maxim's saw the Persian potatoes. They gasped with horror. An Iranian Air Force plane had to fly to Paris to bring back tons of French potatoes. Before the gala dinner began, the Shah and Queen Farah received the international Heads of States one by one. Each paid their respects, either by bowing or, in the case of the ladies, with a curtsey. However, the leaders of the Gulf States – Doha, Dubai, and so on – dressed in their traditional, white robes, laced with gold thread, greeted the Shah by their customary kissing him on each cheek. The Court attendants, patiently waiting to show the guests to their seating places, and seeing the look of disapproval on the Shah's face, found it difficult to keep their own faces straight.

Later, during the meal, the Shah was the one to have a wry smile. The fourth course was peacock, called the "Persian Bird" by Aristotle. In Persia, it is considered the royal bird and engraved on thrones. The Arab chiefs' faces, on seeing the pheasant, went pale, for peacock meat is considered *makruh* – unsavoury and only to be eaten when there is nothing else.

The contrast of the dazzling elegance of the celebration and the living standards of the Shah's people was so great that the world's leaders could not ignore it. Many, including Queen Elizabeth, US President Richard Nixon and French President Georges Pompidou turned down the invitation to attend. Throughout the world, the international press condemned the extravagance. Consequently, opposition to his rule continued to mushroom. Even so, the West continued to give him lukewarm support, afraid of the Soviet Union's territorial ambitions.

However, his wealth was growing rapidly with his 5% take from oil revenue. In 1973, the Arab states imposed an oil embargo on the West as a consequence of Israel's capturing parts of Egypt, Jordan and Syria after the Yom Kippur War. The Shah saw this as an opportunity to persuade OPEC to increase oil prices. In January 1974, the price of a barrel of oil rose from $2.90 to $11.65, almost four times dearer. Consequently, Britain's inflation hit 20%, resulting in electricity blackouts becoming widespread, a three-day working week being imposed, and Prime Minister Edward Heath resigning after losing a general election. US inflation rose to 11.1%. The West realised that Iran was no longer under their heel. The American press was damning the Shah, making play that they saw through his ambition to become the leader of the Persian Gulf Area and the Indian Ocean Basin.

The Shah had led the US to believe that he would never accept communism as long as he ruled. When President Carter's administration took office, they began to see the Shah as troublesome. The UK's Prime Minister, Harold Wilson, and French President Valery Giscard d'Estaing supposedly approached the Shah for a loan.

In 1976, the Shah antagonised the merchants of the bazaars by creating a political monopoly, the *Rastakhiz* or People's Party. Membership was compulsory and swingeing taxes were imposed as there was no longer any worthwhile opposition in the Majlis. A few outspoken opponents were exiled to become stateless citizens. Ironically, the Shah's education policy had produced better-educated young people, but the labour market could not absorb the higher number of educated youngsters. There were three times more universities and literacy had increased from 27% to 80%. When seeing the illiterate having better employment prospects in manual jobs, the elite grew disgruntled. The strict role of Islam in family life was criticised and a more secular approach began to seep in. Their discontent fermented the seeds of a coup that would come to a climax in 1978. Meanwhile, in the countryside, women were still using the local stream to wash clothes using stones.

During the 1960-70s, the Shah had been quietly strengthening his armed forces so that by 1973 he had the fourth biggest army in the world, after China, the US, and the USSR, making him feel impregnable. Queen Farah's extravagance had become endemic. She created a department, staffed by over a hundred civil servants, simply to update the Royal Palaces. Her most extravagant project was the building of an art museum costing over one million dollars, then filling it with millions of dollars worth of paintings from leading contemporary artists. Today, the art collection mostly survives intact in the vaults of the Tehran Museum of Contemporary Art. The building was opened on Farah Diba's birthday in 1977 by Nelson Rockefeller. It contains masterpieces by Francis Bacon, Pablo Picasso, Jackson Pollock, and Auguste Renoir. The collection is now worth as much as three billion dollars. By then, with the Shah calling himself the *Shahanshah*, or King of Kings, his wife's spending was out of control. The Shah's ego knew no bounds. He decided to change the Islamic calendar to his own Persian calendar. The Islamic year 1397 (1977AD), based on the number of years since the flight of Mohammed from Mecca to Medina, became 2567 – the number of years since the birth of King Cyrus.

By September 1978, the widespread demonstrations and rioting had become widespread. On 8th September, at Jaleh Square in Tehran, he used his troops to quell a protest. Approximately 100 were killed and 200 injured. Martial law was imposed, but strikes continued to paralyse the country. Desperate to cling on to power, troops were regularly bussed into Tehran dressed as construction workers in white overalls to provide a cheering crowd for the passing royal motorcade.

Soon after declaring martial law, the Shah was interviewed by *Time Magazine* on Iran's problems. Undertaken in his private office at the Saadabad Palace, he looked ill. His face was gaunt, his manner grim; his eyes portrayed a sad man. Instead of his usual attire of a colourful military uniform, he wore a dark suit with a somber tie. The photograph taken at the interview, almost certainly without him realizing its significance, showed a picture of Soraya on his desk, not his wife, Farah Diba.

Read into this what you will. The interview was given considerable publicity but Soraya doesn't mention it. The question unanswered is whether, in 1950, he truly fell in love with Soraya at first sight or had he been flattered by finding that at thirty-one he could still attract a beautiful, eighteen-year-old virgin.

In December, a march against the regime in Tehran totalled over six million people. By then, even the clerics had gone on strike by refusing to hold Friday services as a sign that they disapproved of the regime. Instead, smuggled cassettes of speeches by Ayatollah Khomeini were being passed around.

On 16th January 1979, the Shah left the country for the last time at the behest of Prime Minister Shapour Bakhtiar; ironically, he was Soraya's uncle. Oddly, no mention of the final events leading to the Shah's overthrow is made in Soraya's second biography.

26

THE CLOSING YEARS

The Shah Dies

Prime Minister Shapour Bakhtiar dissolved SAVAK, freed the political prisoners and allowed Ayatollah Khomeini to return from exile in France. Within weeks, Khomeini's followers had taken control of Tehran. The army declared itself neutral. The Pahlavi dynasty was finished, and the Islamic Republic officially replaced the monarchy on 1st April 1979 with Ayatollah Khomeini as Supreme Head of State.

For what was his second spell in exile, the Shah was initially greeted by President Sadat of Egypt. However, Shah Pahlavi was an ill man and needed prompt surgery for cancer. He moved to Morocco as a guest of King Hassan II who generously gave him and his family diplomatic passports. Realising Soraya's Imperial Iranian passport would no longer be recognised and she would become stateless, the Shah requested one for Soraya. For the rest of her life, Soraya held a Moroccan diplomatic passport; it is not mentioned in her biographies.

The Shah and his family had become an international embarrassment as the Iranian government issued demands for their return. After travelling via the Bahamas and Mexico, the Shah undertook surgery in the United States in late-October with the reluctant agreement of President Jimmy Carter. It was followed by six weeks of recuperation. His prolonged stay in the USA was extremely unpopular in Iran. In an act of revenge, on 4th November 1979, students stormed the American Embassy in Tehran, taking fifty-two hostages. Forced to move to Panama for three months, the Shah eventually accepted permanent asylum in Egypt.

Ardeshir Zahedi, the general's son who had been married to Princess Shahnaz, visited Soraya occasionally in Paris. He told her that the Shah was living in the Koubbeh Palace, a 400-room Italianate palace situated several kilometres north of central Cairo.

Staying in the Koubbeh Palace was a case of *déjà vu* for the ousted Shah. He had stayed there when he was awaiting his wedding to Princess Fawzieh in March 1939. It still remains Egypt's principle guesthouse for visiting foreign dignitaries: Tony Blair and Richard Nixon have stayed there.

It upset Soraya that the Shah was living alone in a 400-room palace. She felt in his debt and briefly had thoughts about visiting him. The Shah died in the Koubbeh Palace on 27th July 1980 from non-Hodgkin lymphoma, aged sixty. Despite the enormity of the Shah's downfall, there is no mention of the revolution, nothing about her Moroccan passport, nothing of the Shah buying her the Paris apartment, nor the subsequent problems that faced the Shah and his family in her second biography. Instead, the Shah's last year in her last biography is an empty, philosophical, somewhat meaningless reflection of her own life. She ponders on still enjoying trees, flowers and animals. Despite her feeling of sadness, she tries to remember the good things of her time as Empress: trying to help others with her charities, the friends she made among the people, and the loyalty she felt for Iran.

Khalil Dies

On the 16th January 1983, Khalil, aged eighty-two, died. In her final biography, this major event in her life is given just four lines. She acknowledged his death had been peaceful in his old age and that she owed him for her strength and pride as a Bakhtiari; furthermore, his belief in being truthful in all things he had thankfully passed on to her.

Given the fact that Khalil had left Persia to study at the University of Berlin, fallen in love with her mother, and returned to Isfahan to persuade his mother that he wished to marry a foreign Christian, then, with his mother's non-active cooperation, he had returned to marry Eva, finished his degree, returned to Isfahan and built a family home, returned to Berlin to please Eva, escaped possible persecution by the Nazis, returned to Isfahan to survive the anti-Bakhtiari oppressive persecution by Reza Shah Pahlavi, became Iran's ambassador to West Germany for thirty years, and supported Soraya's divorce with the words, 'Thank God', a more comprehensive epitaph may have been expected.

Shah's Tomb

In 1987, eight years after the Shah's overthrow, Soraya and her brother, Bijan, took a holiday in Egypt. In Cairo, by chance, they visited the Al Rifa'i mosque. Their guide at one point whispered in Bijan's ear. When Soraya asked what had been said, Bijan told his sister that the Shah's tomb was nearby. The guide had asked whether Soraya would like to see it. As they moved past the vault of ex-King Farouk, a chill passed down her spine. An old man sitting on a carpet in front of the crypt stood and profusely offered his apologies. If he had known, he would have lit candles and found some flowers, he explained.

In the shadows, Soraya saw a simple black slab of marble. Engraved were the words: *Mohammed Reza, Shah of Iran.* She squeezed her brother's hand and wept.

Unlike the first Shah Pahlavi, whose body was returned to Tehran, Soraya's husband would lie eternally in a foreign land. She admitted thinking that the country which he loved so much tore him apart.

The raw fact is that the Shah's extravagance, born of his belief that he was appointed by God to rule, led him to tearing his country apart. On several occasions he could have gone down the path of the European monarchies such as in Britain, where the monarch reigns, but does not rule. He wanted it both ways and to the bitter end illogically defended his hands-on approach. Between his accession in 1941 and his overthrow in 1979, he appointed no fewer than thirty-three changes of prime minister. A total of twenty-four different men held the office; some were appointed more than once. He sacked them whenever their policies didn't suit him. One, Ahmad Qavam, served on three occasions ten years apart between August 1942 and July 1952. By contrast, in Britain during the same period, there were eight, democratically elected, prime ministers.

Loved Twice?

Soraya was fifty-eight when she finished her second biography in 1990. She mused that Mohammed Pahlavi lay in Cairo, while Franco Indovina was in Scilly. She claimed that she loved them both, admitting they were totally different. She quotes two lines from an ancient Persian poem:

Over the tombs of kings leap the gazelles
Over the poets grow the marguerites.

The last sentences of her biography asked the reader how she could be sad when in her heart there were leaping gazelles and a bunch of marguerites.

27

THE FINAL YEARS

The Rapid Decline

Eva died of natural causes in July 1994, aged eighty-eight, and was buried in the simple family grave in Munich next to Khalil. Soraya's best friend passed away peacefully. She was, perhaps, the only person who fully understood the deep psychological scar imposed on her innocent eighteen-year-old daughter. Soraya had gone from being a happy, gifted, unknown student in Switzerland to a queen in a few short months. At the time of Eva's death, Soraya was staying at her Spanish villa, *Maryam*, named after Khalil's mother.

Her mother's death hit Soraya hard. Soraya's health had been detiorating for some time and the last seven years of her life saw a big deterioration according to her cousin. When in Paris during the winter, to escape her loneliness, she continued to find solace with the lifestyle of the idle rich.

The last years, however, saw a rapid decline as the former empress, one of the most photographed women of all time, continued to attend parties given by the younger jet-set. A regular visitor in the bar of the Hotel Plaza Athénée, across the road from her apartment, I was shocked to find several photos taken shortly before her death in 2001, aged sixty-nine. Soraya is barely recognisable from the slim, elegant thirty-one-year old in *The Three Faces*.

In the final chapter of her autobiography, Soraya claims she was lucky enough to have loved two men and asks how many women can say the same. She speculates as to whether she could fall in love again, and hints that she liked the idea. One can only speculate, but her jet-set lifestyle may have been made in the hope that another male companion would come along and sweep her of her feet.

On the 22nd June 2001, her 69th birthday, she was alone with Massimo Gargia, a well-known gigolo, a lover of older women, at the Royal Monceau Hotel Raffles, in Paris. Four months later, she would be dead. Gargia, a fantasist and gigolo, claimed to have bedded countless older women including Greta Garbo, twenty years older than him. That Soraya's final birthday should end with a disreputable, vile, international philanderer is undoubtedly the saddest part of her story.

Sudden Death

Soraya died officially of undisclosed causes in her apartment at 46 Avenue Montaigne, Paris on 25th October 2001. She had gone to bed with a warm drink, served by her live-in maid. Her maid later gave evidence at the inquest that there was nothing wrong with Soraya when they wished each other goodnight. The following morning, the maid had found Soraya lying dead on the floor.

Upon learning of Soraya's death, her brother Bijan immediately drove to Paris from Cologne. He began planning his sister's funeral. Bizarrely, however, he never attended it. Five days later, he died mysteriously in his Paris hotel.

Soraya's funeral took place on 6th November at the American Cathedral in Paris. The mourners included Princess Ashraf, Prince

Courtesy Alamy Images
The family grave in Munich

Reza Pahlavi, the son of Queen Farah and would-be-heir to the Shah's throne. Several members of the Bakhtiari family, including her two cousins, were also present. Her remains, along with those of her brother, were buried in the family grave at Westfriedhof in Munich.

Shortly after her death, the Iranian weekly newspaper *Nimrooz* published an article claiming Soraya and her brother were murdered, but offered no evidence.

The official police verdict was that Soraya died of natural causes. This verdict seems too convenient, as the history of the French police satisfactorily solving murders of foreigners is littered with expedient explanations. There was the death of Sir Jack Drummond and his family in the Alpes-de-Haute-Provence in 1952 – the famous Dominici affair. Then Fiona Jones from Birmingham was killed as she cycled through countryside north of Paris in 1989. It took her strong-willed husband haranguing the police to get justice years later. In 2012, three members of a British family were shot near Lake Annecy;

no one has been charged. In 2020, Esther Dingley, aged 37 from Durham, went missing while hiking alone in the Pyrenees. There has been no satisfactory resolution of the mystery, despite some of her bones being found in 2021.

The Auction

Soraya's possessions, excluding her Paris and Marbella properties, were auctioned in Paris by the auctioneers Druot-Montaigne. The sale was scheduled to run for three days from 29ᵗʰ–31ˢᵗ May 2002. However, the interest generated by Soraya's death forced the organisers to stage a pre-exhibition. The auction house was decorated with roses to conjure up the atmosphere of a Persian garden. In her will, she left instructions for her personal possessions to be auctioned and the proceeds from the sale to be bequeathed to her favourite charities: the International Red Cross, and various children's and animal charities. The display of jewellery, silverware, watches, furniture, paintings, carpets, furs, evening dresses, rare photos, and a Silver Spur Rolls Royce stunned the public. Over one thousand articles were exhibited. The auction aroused unparalleled interest, and the sentimental value of the objects generally increased their material value.

The most flattering of her portraits fetched well over US $250,000. One object above all others conjured memories of the young princess – her splendid Christian Dior wedding dress. It fetched US $1.2 million. Hundreds of unpublished photos bound in leather albums bore testimony to Soraya's fabulous life. Studio portraits by Harcourt and others flattered her eyes, lips and dark hair. Professional photos of her State visits to Europe, Russia and America sold rapidly. Personal snaps of her horse-riding along the Caspian Sea, laughing with the Shah on a picnic, or with him on the ski slopes were soon sold.

Her jewelry included her engagement ring– the solitaire diamond weighing 22.37 carats. Her platinum and sapphire necklace, an exact copy of that worn at her wedding, and designed by the Italian jeweler Bulgari, raised US $1 million. A gold cigarette case bearing the Pahlavi Crown, an Asprey and Gerrard toilette service, a Boucheron diamond watch, a ruby and emerald brooch given to Soraya on her honeymoon sold rapidly. The wardrobe collection bore testament to her glamorous lifestyle. It included the white mink cape worn by Soraya on her wedding day. All her clothes proved popular and seen as an investment.

On the last day of the sale, Iranian exiles bought many of the Persian rugs. The 1985 Rolls Royce Silver Spur went for over US $59,000, four times its catalogue price. Piece by piece over the three days, Soraya's private life was auctioned away, raising more than US $8.6 million. All that was left was the smell of the roses.

Controversial Will

Soraya's two properties in Paris and Malaga were conservatively valued at $30 million each. They had been left by Soraya in her will to her brother. However, because of his sudden demise five days after Soraya's death, the money was passed to the German state government of North Rhine-Westphalia, where her brother had lived. Bijan had died without making a will. The German authorities appealed for anyone related to Bijan, who might be entitled to his estate, to come forward. Some fifty claims were made. All were found to be impostors. One man produced documents that appeared to claim he was Bijan's illegitimate son. DNA tests carried out after Bijan's body was exhumed proved the claim was false.

The Cologne Higher Regional Court agreed that the proceeds of the auction in Paris could be distributed to her nominated charities. However, the remaining assets, as a result of the sale of her two properties, were disputed in court until 2016. The problems centred around whether a note, supposedly written by Bijan before he died, nominating his chauffeur and private secretary as his heir was a fake. Soraya's will had stipulated if Bijan pre-deceased her, the residue should go to her nominated charities. As Bijan did not pre-decease her, in the end Soraya's bequest eventually ended up paying for street lighting, rubbish collection and other public amenities in North Rhine-Westphalia.

28

POSSIBLE OR PROBABLE

Whether in America, Britain, the Soviet Union or Switzerland, there was agreement on one fact: Soraya's meetings with the world's leading gynaecologists drew the same conclusion. Soraya was neither born barren nor had become infertile as a result of being given aureomycin to help cure her typhoid. The official medical opinion was always, "Everything will be all right; there is nothing wrong with Soraya's fertility."

A Russian gynaecologist claimed the Shah was the source of the problem. The Shah, however, had had serious internal problems. Acute appendicitis was described by his American surgeons as, "A rare and unusual case." His duodenum ulcers were kept secret within his family for years until they became critical. His sexual relations with many different lovers before meeting Soraya raised the possibility of his having acquired venereal disease. Finally, there was the rumour in Court circles, that I garnered from Soraya's cousin, that he had problems with erectile dysfunction.

The question has to be asked, if the world's leading gynaecologists all agreed there was no physical problem with Soraya, then what was the matter?

Did the Shah remain in love with Soraya until his death; after all, as late as 1978, the only photo on his desk was that of Soraya.

During the years after Soraya had left Tehran, the Shah's use of call girls from Paris increased. He reputedly had sometimes two in bed at the same time. His unfaithfulness was common knowledge within the Court circle. It is conceivable that his third wife, Farah, knew and consequently remained sexually active with her former fiancé.

By blaming Soraya for a lack of an heir, the Pahlavis were covering up the Shah's problems that were common knowledge in the Court.

If Farah's four children were fathered by her lover, then her first son, Prince Reza, would not have been the legitimate heir to the throne. The Pahlavi dynasty would have collapsed despite their best efforts to hang on to the Iranian throne.

The Pahlavis belief that the Shah's rule was determined in the stars, thus preventing one of the Shah's half-brothers from becoming the Shah, caused the divorce that destroyed a dynasty.

Courtesy Alamy Images
'I think you were in love with her'
'Mmm… perhaps?!'

BIBLIOGRAPHY

Walter Krause: *Soraya, Queen of Persia*, (Macdonald 1956).

Princess Soraya Esfandiary Bakhtiary, translated by Constantine Fitzgibbon: *Soraya, The Autobiography of Her Imperial Highness*, (Doubleday & Company 1963).

Princess Soraya Esfandiary Bakhtiary: *Palace of Solitude*, translated by Hubert Gibbs (Quartet Books Ltd 1992).

Patricia Baker: *Iran The Bradt Travel* Guide, (The Globe Pequot Press Inc).

Farzaneh Milani: *Words not Swords, Iranian Women Writers and the Freedom of Movement*, (Syracuse University Press 2011).

Jaam-e-Jam: *Secrets of the Iranian Revolution, Televisions Open Forum*, translated by Doki Bibiyan (Xlibris 2010).

Fiona Ross: *Dining with the Rich and the Royals*, (Rowman & Littlefield 2016).

Sir Anthony Parsons: *The Pride and Fall: Iran 1974-1979*, (Jonathon Cape 1984).

Charles Wighton: *The Australian Women's Weekly*, 17 July 1957.

Robert Feldman: *Life Magazine*, 12 May 1958.

Ervard Abrahamian: *The Coup* (The New Press, New York 2013).

Bernews.com, 29 December 2013.

New York Times 23 July 1952: *World Court Bars Ruling on Iran Oil.*

Minutes of the 562nd Meeting of UN Security Council, 17th October 1951, Chapter VIII: *Maintenance of International Peace and Security - The Anglo-Iranian Oil Crisis.*

Iran Review, 6th June 2016.

Malcolm Byrne: *The Secret CIA History of the Iran Coup, 1953,* (George Washington University).

Farah Pahlavi: *An Enduring Love: My Life with the Shah - A Memoir,* (Hyperion 2005.)

Darius Kadivar: *Stardust Memories - Princess Soraya's Hollywood Temptations* (IC Publications April 2007)

Francesco Terracina: *L'ulitmo volo per Punta Raisi. Sciagura o Strage?*

VB.com/Soraya

trove.nia.gov.au

Myspace.com/soraya

Madeeha Syed's blog 15 June 2014

New York Times January 10th 1979

The Washington Post January 17th 1979

13 03 JUE 17:14 FAX 082 861407
Notaire en second

JOLIS ABOGADOS
Notaire en second

int :

Présent :

1991

27 Juin.

Testament

de

Princesse Soraya

rdiari Pakhevai

COMPTE N°

COMPTE N° 102313 K

115 311 R

et H. MOREL d'ARLEUX et Th. du BOŸS

NOTAIRES

15, rue des Saints-Pères - 75006 PARIS

6 JUIL 1991

Hervé MOREL d'ARLEUX et Thierry du BOYS

Notaires associés

15, Rue des Saints-Pères – 75006 PARIS

LEPHONE : 01.42.60.34.60
X : 01.42.96.38.47
sse email : stmstintsperes@paris.notaires.fr

SOLIS
Abogados
Jacinto Benavente 4
Edificio Las Gaviotas 6°1
29600 MARBELLA (Malaga)
ESPAGNE

'CCESSION PRINCESSE SORAYA ESFANDIARI BAKHTIARI
AA/AVN/

sier suivi par : Me MOREL d'ARLEUX   PARIS, le 26 février 2003

Mon Cher Maître,

En votre qualité de représentant de l'Association pour la Protection des animaux abandonnés, je vous confirme que je suis chargé du règlement de la succession de la Princesse Soraya ESFANDIARI BAKHTIARI, décédée à PARIS le 25 octobre 2001. Vous trouverez sous ce pli copie de son testament fait en la forme authentique en date du 27 juin 1991.

En ma qualité d'exécuteur testamentaire, et conformément à la mission que la Princesse Soraya m'a fixé, je souhaite nommer cette Association comme bénéficiaire des dispositions prises par cette dernière en faveur d'une association de protection des animaux.

En conséquence, je vous saurais gré de bien vouloir m'adresser :
- les statuts de l'Association,
- le décret reconnaissant votre association d'utilité publique,
- les modalités d'autorisation à recevoir ce legs,
- le pouvoir de son représentant.

A toutes fins utiles, je vous précise que l'actif successoral en Espagne se compose essentiellement de parts de SARL propriétaire d'une maison à MARBELLA, actuellement en cours de vente.

Enfin, je vous conseille vivement de contacter Maître Anne FORCE, Avocate à FRANKFURT (60313   Allemagne) Stiftstrasse 9-17, qui pourra représenter efficacement vos intérêts.

Restant à votre entière disposition,

Je vous prie de croire, Monsieur, en l'expression de mes sentiments distingués.

Société Titulaire d'un Office Notarial
Membre d'une association agréée. Le règlement des honoraires par chèque est accepté

" réalisations.

" Après réglement des droits de succession, ainsi
" que des frais et honoraires , le produit net de ces réalisations
" sera déposé sur un compte spécial ouvert au nom de "SUCCESSION
" PRINCESSE SORAYA ESFANDIARI BAKHTIARI" dans les livres de la
" Banque SCHWEIZERISCHE BANK GESEILCHAFT, Banhoff Strass à ZURICH
" (Suisse). Ces fonds seront investis en valeurs mobilières .
" Seuls les revenus de cet investissement, seront versés à mon
" Frère BIJAN ESFANDIARI BAKHTIARI, sa vie durant. Celui-ci ne
" pourra en aucun cas utiliser le capital .

" A son décès, ces fonds reviendront à son ou ses
" enfants légitimes, au regard de la Législation Allemande, ou
" à défaut aux Associations suivantes et dans les proportions
" ci-après :

" UN TIERSà la SOCIETE PROTECTRICE DES ANIMAUX "
" établie en France,
" UN TIERSà l' ASSOCIATION DES PARALYSES DE FRANCE
" et plus spécialement aux Enfants Handicapés dont se préoccupe
" cette Association,
" UN TIERSà la CROIX ROUGE FRANCAISE établie en
" FRANCE.

" Les dispositions ci-dessus s'appliqueront exac-
" tement de la même manière , sauf la désignation des bénéfi-
" ciaires ci-après.

" I°/ A tous les biens que je pourrai posséder au
" jour de mon décès sur le Territoire ALLEMAND , et notamment
" la maison que je possède dans ce Pays, située à MUNICH Opitz
" Strass N°16, MUNICH 19. Bien entendu, ma Mère Madame Eva
" ESFANDIARI BAKHTIARI, née KARL continuera sa vie Durant
" de bénéficier de l'usufruit de cette maison .

" 2°/ A tous les biens que je pourrai posséder au
" jour de mon décès, en ESPAGNE, directement ou indirectement,

" En ce qui concerne les bénéficiaires dans ces deux
" Pays,(Allemagne et Espagne), les fonds à provenir de la vente
" reviendront dans les mêmes conditions que pour mes biens en
" France, savoir

" I/ Pour les biens situés en ALLEMAGNE,

" UN TIERS à la SOCIETE PROTECTRICE DES ANIMAUX existant
" en ALLEMAGNE,
" UN TIERSà une Association d'enfants Handicapés
" que désignera mon exécuteur testamentaire,
" UN TIERSà la CROIX ROUGE ALLEMANDE/

S.E.B

"2/ Pour les biens situés en ESPAGNE . Directement
ou indirectement :
        " UN TIERS à la SOCIETE PROTECTRICE DES ANIMAUX
" établie en ESPAGNE,
        " UN TIERS à une Association d'enfants handicapés
que désignera mon exécuteur testamentaire .
        " UN TIERS à la CROIX ROUGE ESPAGNOLE.

        "Je révoque toutes dispositions antérieures."

        Ce testament a été dicté par la testatrice à Me
MOREL d'ARLEUX , qui l'a fait écrire à la MACHINE A ECRIRE
par Madame MONTAUBERY sa secrétaire, tel qu'il lui a été dicté
puis Me MOREL d'ARLEUX l'a lu à la Testatrice, qui a déclaré
que ce testament est l'expression exacte de ses volontés, et
qu'elle persévère dans ces dispositions.

        Fait et passé à Paris, sixième arrondissement,
rue des Saints Pères N° 15, au deuxième étage . dans le bureau
personnel de Me MOREL d'ARLEUX Notaire,

        Le VINGT SEPT JUIN MIL NEUF CENT QUATRE VINGT ONZE
A quatorze heures trente minutes.

        Et la Testatrice a signé avec les Notaires après
une nouvelle lecture entière des présentes, le tout en la pré-
sence non interrompue de Me BARATTE Notaire.

S.E.B.

Appendix

REALISATION (OF THE WILL)

After the rules of succession and costs, the net remaining assets will be deposited in a special account 'Successors of Princess Soraya ...' in the accounts of the Banque S B G in Zurich, Switzerland. The funds will be invested in real estate. Only the revenues from this investment will benefit her brother S E B during his lifetime. In no event will he have access to the investment capital. On his death the investment will be intended for his legitimate children according to German Law. Or in the event this does not apply the funds will be distributed as follows:

- One third to the Protection of Animals Society in France.
- One third to the Association for the Paralysed in France with an emphasis on children.
- One third to the Red Cross in France.

The disbursements below are to be applied in the same way, except for the beneficiaries stated below.
- 1st All my possessions at my time of death located in Germany

and specifically the house I owm In Munich No 16 ... Naturally my mother Madame Eve E B born Karl can continue to live in the house in her lifetime.

2nd All the possessions that I might have when I die located in Spain.

As far as the beneficiaries in those two countries (Germany and Spain), the funds from the sale will be treated in the same way as my assets in France, thus:

-1   For the assets in Germany:
One third for the Protection of Animals Society.
One third for the Association for Handicapped Children specified by my executor.
One third to the German Red Cross.

-2   For the assets in Spain:
One third for the Protection of Animals established in Spain.
One third to an Association for Handicapped Children s specified by my executor.
One third to the Spanish Red Cross.

All previous Wills are annulled.

It then states who prepared the Will and the address of the solicitor in Paris.

Dated 27 Sept 1991.

The missing pages 4 and 5 could be significant. No mention is made of her assets in France.

=

This book is printed on paper from sustainable sources managed under the Forest Stewardship Council (FSC) scheme.

It has been printed in the UK to reduce transportation miles and their impact upon the environment.

For every new title that Troubador publishes, we plant a tree to offset CO_2, partnering with the More Trees scheme.

For more about how Troubador offsets its environmental impact, see www.troubador.co.uk/sustainability-and-community

QUEEN SORAYA

HER DIVORCE
DESTROYED A DYNASTY

Getty image

NOVELS BY R W KAY

A Nastia Game – hardback published 2009, paperback 2013
Bin Laden's Nemesis – published 2012
Iraq's Retribution – published 2014
The World Is Empty – published 2016
Prohibited Portrait – published 2019

QUEEN
SORAYA

HER DIVORCE
DESTROYED A DYNASTY

R W KAY

Troubador Publishing Ltd
Unit E2 Airfield Business Park
Harrison Road, Market Harborough
Leicestershire LE16 7UL
Tel: 0116 279 2299
Email: books@troubador.co.uk
Web: www.troubador.co.uk

ISBN 978 1 83628 459 8

British Library Cataloguing in Publication Data.
A catalogue record for this book is available from the British Library.

The manufacturer's authorised representative in the EU for product safety is Authorised Rep
Compliance Ltd, 71 Lower Baggot Street, Dublin D02 P593 Ireland (www.arccompliance.com).

Printed and bound by CPI Group (UK) Ltd, Croydon, CR0 4YY
Typeset in 12pt Minion Pro by Troubador Publishing Ltd, Leicester, UK

MIX
Paper | Supporting
responsible forestry
FSC® C013604
FSC
www.fsc.org

DEDICATION

The book is dedicated to all Iranians who remember with fondness,
and/or accept, that in the seven years of Queen Soraya's reign, she
single-handedly improved the standard of living of the residents in Iran.